W9-AEW-776

AUTOCRACY AND REVOLUTION
IN RUSSIA

THE MACMILLAN COMPANY
NEW YORK · BOSTON · CHICAGO · DALLAS
ATLANTA · SAN FRANCISCO

MACMILLAN & CO., Limited
LONDON · BOMBAY · CALCUTTA
MELBOURNE

THE MACMILLAN CO. OF CANADA, Ltd.
TORONTO

p. 26

DK265
K6

AUTOCRACY AND REVOLUTION IN RUSSIA

BY

BARON SERGIUS A. KORFF, D.C.L., LL.D.

PROFESSOR OF POLITICAL SCIENCE, SCHOOL OF FOREIGN SERVICE, GEORGE-
TOWN UNIVERSITY, WASHINGTON, D. C. SOMETIME PROFESSOR
OF RUSSIAN LAW AND HISTORY, UNIVERSITY OF
HELSINGFORS, FINLAND, AND WOMEN'S
UNIVERSITY OF PETROGRAD, RUSSIA

MACMILLAN AND CO., LIMITED
ST. MARTIN'S STREET, LONDON
1923

JUN 1965

98449

PRINTED IN THE UNITED STATES OF AMERICA

COPYRIGHT, 1923,

BY THE NORTHWESTERN UNIVERSITY

Set up and printed. Published April, 1923.

Press of
J. J. Little & Ives Company
New York, U. S. A.

THE N. W. HARRIS LECTURES

were founded in 1906 through the generosity of Mr. Norman Wait Harris of Chicago, and are to be given annually. The purpose of the lecture foundation is, as expressed by the donor, "to stimulate scientific research of the highest type and to bring the results of such research before the students and friends of Northwestern University, and through them to the world. By the term 'scientific research' is meant scholarly investigation into any department of human thought or effort without limitation to research in the so-called natural sciences, but with a desire that such investigation should be extended to cover the whole field of human knowledge."

PREFACE

It was with much hesitation that I accepted the honor to deliver the Harris lectures during the present month, because I felt that it would be extremely difficult to give in the space of six lectures an adequate picture of the complex processes of the Russian Revolution. Much of the scientific and historical material still remains untouched, neither analyzed nor systematized. However, we know enough at present to discern at least the main lines of development of the social forces that brought about the Revolution.

I suppose that most educated people realize that the Revolution did not come suddenly and quite unexpectedly, but that it was the necessary outcome of the social readjustment that was taking place in Russia during the three last decades. Thus, in order to make the picture of the events of 1917 more comprehensible, I had to start my narrative with the preceding period, when autocracy was gradually falling to pieces, when the old régime was no longer able to satisfy the needs and requirements of social life and when the political system of Tsarism began rapidly to degenerate, becoming demoralized and utterly inefficient.

There were many warnings of the coming social storm, but none were stronger and more vital than the disturbances of 1905, that followed the defeat of the Japanese war. Alas! that sad lesson was not learned by the Russian government. The chances of the October Constitution were lost; the ruling classes, demoralized as they were, did not want to give in and fought for a hopeless cause defending the dying autocracy. This necessarily brought about the Revolution.

I must express in conclusion my feelings of deep gratitude to the Committee of the Harris Foundation for having given me this opportunity to discuss some of the historical lessons provided by the Russian Revolution. My personal thanks are also due to my friend, Mr. Arthur D. Call, for his valuable suggestions and cordial help, and to Professor Theodore W. Koch, Secretary of the Harris Lecture Committee, for his untiring assistance and friendly advice.

S. A. K.

April 10th, 1922.
Northwestern University,
Evanston, Ill.

CONTENTS

	PAGE
AUTOCRACY	1
THE RUSSIAN PEASANT	29
THE RUSSO-JAPANESE WAR	56
THE EVENTS OF THE REVOLUTION	80
GERMANY AND THE RUSSIAN REVOLUTION	104
SOME LESSONS OF THE RUSSIAN REVOLUTION	130
INDEX	157

AUTOCRACY AND REVOLUTION
IN RUSSIA

AUTOCRACY AND THE REVOLUTION IN RUSSIA

CHAPTER I

AUTOCRACY

I

DURING the last decades preceding the Revolution of 1917 it became constantly more evident to attentive observers that Russian autocracy was doomed. It was a dying régime, gradually degenerating and decaying from within, whose days were already numbered, like a person with some deadly disease lingering on under the influence of oxygen.

Unfortunately among the Russian ruling classes there were many men who were stubbornly clinging to power, artificially prolonging the régime by making all sorts of compromises; some among them were selfishly arguing that every extra day in power was a gain to themselves. The most important historical conclusion that one can draw from these last years of autocracy is that, as a political principle, it was not able to save itself by compromise; as soon as concessions to opposite sides were started, autocracy was doomed, its very backbone being broken by such concessions.

1

But before we analyze the situation in Russia created by the process of the decay of autocracy, it is necessary to define the term itself. What is autocracy after all, and why was it dying in Russia since the end of the nineteenth century?

Autocracy as a form of government has two sides to it: first, it is a political system of government, and, secondly, it has a certain social background on which such a political system has historically grown up and developed. The first is a judicial, outward frame for the second, its social content.

Autocracy is usually said to be a "one-man-rule," which is a clear but not sufficient definition. As a matter of fact, there never existed anywhere a government in which one single man was the only ruler of a people. Not even the Mongol or other Eastern conquerors ruled absolutely single-handed; there always existed, supporting and assisting them, at least a small group or caste which derived direct advantages out of this rule. As time went on, these social privileges crystallized into a stable social order on which the chief or autocrat could lean, but on which at the same time he was necessarily dependent. When for some reason the ruling group became unstable, whether on account of inner dissatisfaction or because of having lost its contact and bonds with the rest of the people, the position of the autocrat in consequence was weakened; he gradually but steadily lost his powers and finally had to succumb, usually pulling down with him, like Samson in the Temple, the whole social order that formerly created and supported him. Thus, sociologically, autocracy invariably was based on the supremacy of a numerically very small social group called the ruling class, very exclusive and most egotistic, having at its head one man. And it was the will of this man that was considered to embody and represent the will of the whole people. The more exclusive such a social class would become, the longer it was able to keep the power in its own hands.

From the legal point of view, the will of such an autocrat was the supreme power of the social organization, tribe, nation or state; he was the head of this form of government called autocracy, the will of one man being the supreme power. It could maintain itself only as long as the rest of the people submitted blindly to such a rule. Sooner or later, however, would come a day when some other classes or social groups would begin to claim participation in the ruling function. In most cases this meant the end of autocracy, or at least a transition to the establishment of a new form of government. Education, enlightenment and contact with higher civilizations and cultures were always the deciding factors that called forth such claims of other social groups.

With the spread of civilization in modern times, autocracy as a form of government became steadily less possible for social reasons. The ruling class encountered gradually more difficulties and impediments, and was not able to maintain its exclusiveness. But as soon as other classes were admitted to participation in the administration, autocracy had to give way to some other form of government, because the will of the single man at the head of the social organization, the autocrat, was hence effectively limited by all sorts of legal restrictions. The latter were directed towards the limiting of the single will and establishing instead the participation of activities of other persons.

The social life of a people is always fluctuant and very flexible; it is constantly changing, growing, developing, adapting itself to new conditions and surroundings. Yet the social order under which a people live, its form of government, is something more or less stable, being the product of social life crystallized into definite and legal forms. It has sometimes been compared to a crust of a cake, giving social life a certain outward stability and determining its outward shape and appearance. Under this crust the social life continues its further development. It is never stagnant unless national decay sets in and the social body begins to degenerate. In other words, under the cover of the outward form of government, social fermentation and evolution continually go on. At times, however, this fermentation creates social processes that call for further expansion. In such cases the outward crust ceases to satisfy the inner social order and has to give way to the pressure coming from within. When the pressure increases and the crust can no more respond to it, it is usually broken up, bursting open in some cases with extreme violence. In the latter instance we have a revolution, breaking and shattering a former political system in order to give vent to the social forces that have developed beneath the political crust and inside the social body of a people.

Now, of all the forms of government, autocracy is the least flexible and adaptable, the reason being the above-mentioned principle of exclusiveness regulating its social functions. As soon as the required exclusiveness of the ruling class disappears, autocracy is fatally doomed. The new classes, coming to power, prevent the former exclusive rule of one group from persisting. Thus the coming to power of new groups necessarily disintegrates the former ruling group and curtails the powers of its head or chief.

II

Just such social processes were taking place in Russia during the nineteenth century. The political structure, as it crystallized in Russia during the preceding century and in the first half of the nineteenth century, was an autocracy. The nation was ruled and represented by the will of one single man, the Tsar. Only such measures or acts of government could become law and only such acts of State were deemed to represent the will of the Russian people as had previously received the sanction of the Tsar.

It is a great question, however, in all autocracies if that logical assumption can be reversed and the complementing principle also recognized, namely, that all the expressions of the will of the autocrat are *eo ipso* to be regarded as law, creating obligations and duties for the people. There were cases in olden days when Asiatic despots tried to go as far as that; but with the growth of civilization it was found impossible to carry the autocratic principle to its logical conclusion, *ad absurdum*. In Russia even the extreme ideologists of autocracy never dared to assert this latter principle, though the first one, that of all laws and acts of State requiring the exclusive sanction of the Tsar, was unhesitatingly and always accepted.

In the nineteenth century Russia came into close contact with the outside world and began to imbibe at least some of the Western ideas of government. Hence these new ideas could no longer be kept away from the knowledge of the Russian people. They had the first glimpse of them during the wars with Napoleon. In 1812 the Russian armies followed upon the heels of the French and spent several years in Western Europe. The officers who came home after the restoration of the Bourbons realized the defects of the government system in Russia, and consequently hoped for liberal and constitutional improvements. In December, 1825, on account of some troubles that arose in the question of the succession to the throne, the more radical elements of the younger generation even tried to bring about a forcible change in the government system; but they did not find any support in their social surroundings and, therefore, necessarily failed. This episode is known as the December revolt.

The Crimean War provided the next shock to the system. Again educated Russians, having come in closer contact with the Western countries, realized the serious defects of the Russian autocracy. This time the discontent spread in much wider circles of the nation. The Crimean defeat helped along the same lines, bringing to the people a strong proof of how badly the government system was working. The government and ruling class lost their heads and plainly felt that they had no backing in the nation. Besides, there existed a strong group among the government officials

themselves who openly advocated reforms and concessions. The Tsar, Alexander II, was inclined to grant
liberal reforms for the improvement of the government system. He was, in particular, very eager to
emancipate the Russian serfs, being firmly convinced
that serfdom had become extremely harmful to Russia
and was one of the conspicuous causes of the Crimean
disaster.

For a short while the liberal group, having the
sympathies of the Tsar, had the leading influence in
the government during the second half of the fifties
and thus was able to work out several very important
and liberal reform bills. These men, by the law of
March 4, 1861, succeeded in emancipating the serfs
and established a new system of local self-government,
built on very liberal principles; this was the origin of
the zemstvos of 1864. At the same time they reor-
ganized in 1864 the Courts-of-Law on the model of the
French Courts. This was also the real beginning of
the Russian liberal movement, as the reforms brought
to the front of political life the best and most educated
men Russia ever had, a generation that we are still
proud of because of its brilliant and self-sacrificing
achievements.

But the form of government, autocracy, and its
social background still remained unchanged, though
for the moment badly shaken. The Tsar's will was
still the ultimate and supreme power in the Russian
Empire, as there existed no vestige of any constitution
or parliament. On the contrary, the government became afraid of the very words "constitution" and
"parliament," going to the ridiculous extreme of pro-

hibiting even the use of them. The daily press, for example, was forbidden to mention the word constitution in connection with Russia!

The social structure of the Empire also remained as of old. Some new forces did appear, but they were not able to change matters appreciably.

The little they did accomplish in the decade of 1856–1866 was thwarted, distorted and curtailed during the years that followed, because the reactionary party once more had the upper hand. As a result, many of the new liberal institutions became warped and disfigured. In the seventies the ruling classes were already advocating the return to the "happy" times of Nicholas I, when unmitigated autocracy reigned supreme.

This baneful reversion came about in the following way. The liberal movement of the fifties necessarily had its own extremists, especially among the younger people, who had no patience to wait for the slow evolutionary processes, for instance, of the growth of local self-government and for the development of better conditions of living among the peasantry. They expected and advocated revolutionary changes instead, preferring to bring about constitutionalism by simply pulling down the government structure. This naturally alarmed very much the ruling classes and the government. They were in no way prepared to give up their positions, so they retaliated by starting ruthless persecutions, imprisoning, punishing, exiling the young people. The latter in turn began to denounce everything the government did as reactionary, hypocritical and insincere, believing that nothing but personal intimidation could force liberal reforms to be granted.

Thus there started the frightful theory that murder and assassination of representatives of the government were the only means by which constitutionalism in Russia could be established. The higher the official sentenced to be murdered, the better it seemed, because of the greater impression that it might produce on the rest of the government. The Tsar himself was held responsible for the reactionary change that came over the government in the sixties, and soon the revolutionaries began a regular hunt after him. The fiercer the prosecutions became, the worse the revolutionary movement developed. It was a typical vicious circle, but the most astounding fact in this game of mutual extermination was the evident sympathy and support that the idea of murder and assassination of government representatives was finding among the nation at large. The masses as well as the educated people were nearly always on the side of the revolutionaries, condoning their acts of murder and winking at their immorality.

In consequence, a whole generation grew up morally hardened by justifying certain forms of murder. No doubt they had many good qualities, but these were coupled with a terrible point of view. It was intense humanitarianism, but showed a strange lack of respect for human life. There was an enthusiastic attachment to the people and absolute self-denial, but brutal contempt for an opponent's ideas. There was ethical fervor, constant devotion to and firm belief in social redemption, but very shortsighted and immoral participation in a terrific gamble, a gamble with human life; a fight for freedom by assassination, tre-

mendous personal sacrifice, but with, on the whole,
very meager results. We can't wonder that the effects
were meager, notwithstanding the superhuman effort
of the revolutionaries, because of the very wrong moral
foundations of their political fight. It ended sadly in
the murder of the Tsar, Alexander II, the liberator of
the Russian serfs, the most liberal monarch and savior
of the Balkan Slavs. He was hunted down and blown
to pieces by a revolutionary bomb hurled at him on
March 13, 1881.

Murder, however, whatever may be its justification,
never can achieve any good results. It invariably calls
for moral atonement. This is perhaps one of the
greatest moral principles of human life which the
Russian revolutionaries, exasperated by the shortsighted policy of the autocratic government, never
sufficiently appreciated, calling upon themselves by
their own moral limitations the worst punishment. The
ultimate outcome, instead of bringing Russia the
hoped-for freedom, was a worse reaction. It called
forth a government much stronger, more ruthless and
still more reactionary than the one of Alexander II.

The ruling class, the government officials, the Tsar
and his family saw very clearly what tremendous
dangers were threatening them from the discontented
groups. They knew that the social dissatisfaction was
spreading everywhere, making dangerous headway;
but they were in no way willing to give up their own
position, privileges, and advantages. They saw only
the immoral side of the revolutionary movement, the
killing and shooting; not realizing that a social readjustment was proceeding back of it. They attributed

the immorality to wicked propaganda and personal motives.

Thus there started in Russia a fatal duel between two formidable and ruthless opponents, a life-and-death struggle that was bound to bring disaster to the nation. Autocracy, having lost its social support, was fighting to save itself; but calling forth by this only worse and more extreme forms of radicalism. This is the historical meaning of the three decades preceding the Great War of 1914. It was the display of the last effort of autocracy to prolong its existence, fighting for it against constantly increasing odds and enemies.

The reign of Alexander III, 1881–1894, was the climax of reaction. It rightly might have seemed to the outside world that autocracy was at the height of its power and glory. Only very few contemporaries realized the dangers of the inner situation in Russia and knew that the government was not as secure and strong as it appeared to foreign observers. They alone saw the dark clouds, yet far distant, on the political horizon; but their knowledge was based on a sound reasoning. They were arguing that new forms of government were developing in the West, and that Russia in the long run could not cut herself away from Europe. Sooner or later the relations with Western Europe had to undermine the Russian form of government. Autocracy could not meet the requirements of modern times, and it had to be replaced by some new form. But these men, arguing thus, were a very small exception and had hardly any influence on public life in Russia.

It was only during the next reign, that of the much

weaker Tsar, Nicholas II, that the real fight of autocracy began, ending in the catastrophe of 1917.

III

It is very important for the impartial analysis of
the situation in Russia during the last twenty years
to keep in mind a clear picture of the social background
of the great death struggle of autocracy.

What were the ruling groups or classes at that time,
and how were they fighting for their social and economic interests?

The ruling classes were composed of two main
groups: the nobility and the bureaucracy, both
gradually differentiating into smaller parts.

The nobility of Russia was in turn divided into the
aristocracy, the most privileged, standing nearest to
the throne and being its principal social support, and
the landed nobility of lower ranks, which was in Russia
much more democratic than in the Western countries.
Among the aristocracy many prided themselves on having long lines of ancestry, going back to the Middle
Ages, the Tartars, or the Moscow princes. This group,
however, never succeeded in maintaining its exclusiveness because the Tsars always jealously kept in their
own hands the power of creating nobles by granting
them estates, titles and class privileges. There existed,
in consequence, a steady influx of new elements, coming from the ranks of the people, and introduced into
the aristocracy through the favor of the Tsar. Among
the lower ranks of nobility this influx was naturally
much stronger and more effective.

Toward the end of the nineteenth century there were very many prominent officials, government servants, ministers and counselors who had risen from the ranks of the people only because their personal ability had caught the favor of some emperor. For that reason the bureaucracy gradually began to overshadow the hereditary nobility, becoming steadily more powerful and influential. From the sociological point of view, bureaucracy is a very unsteady, fluctuating and rather incoherent class. Personal ambitions and ability from below and government favor and selection from above produce constant changes. Still, bureaucracy is a class by itself. It has some social cohesion and sometimes develops even a certain *esprit de corps,* possessing mutual interests and ideals that bind its members together and force upon them a certain unity of policy.

It was by no means the whole class of bureaucracy, however, that was actively participating in the government policies and supporting autocracy. Only the upper strata of bureaucracy were taking part in the shaping of government policies; the rest of the officials, the vast majority of them, simply played the rôle of cogs in the government machine, giving their lives and services for modest salaries, performing unimportant duties, and often not sympathizing with the autocratic ideals of the government they were serving. This was perhaps one of the most conspicuous dangers for autocracy in Russia. It could not rely on its own servants, who were ready to bolt at the first opportunity, and, as a matter of fact, did so very early in the Revolution.

One could often see in autocratic Russia of former

days minor officials thwarting the policy of the government because they did not sympathize with the régime. It was most evident during the last decades of autocracy; very many minor government representatives were absolutely opposed to the policy of persecutions and were trying to save the lives of revolutionaries, giving asylum to fugitives from courts and prisons, assisting them to escape from punishment and in some cases even to evade law and police orders. The sympathies of these minor officials were openly with the people and against the government. The reason for this was that these men felt that the autocratic system was injurious to the nation. Still, they were forced to compromise. They could not resign from the government service, as it was their only source of income. They were ill adapted to the hardships of the struggle for existence, having spent all their lives in the bureaus, typewriting and copying. They were not used to independent action and were afraid of open competition in private life.

Quite different was the position among the higher ranks of the Russian bureaucracy. Here we find power and glory, large incomes and great advantages coupled with various legal and social privileges. It was a distinct success for a man to rise from the lower bureaucratic ranks and penetrate into the small circle of high officials, ministers and counselors of the Tsar, who shared the advantages of their position with those of the highest aristocracy. In such cases it happened often that the aristocrats seemed subservient, endeavoring to acquire new privileges, grants of money and other aid from the high bureaucrats in power.

Toward the end of the nineteenth century, for instance, there developed a gradual impoverishment of the Russian aristocracy. In consequence, its members were keen to receive the assistance of the government and often did not hesitate to ask the ministers of the Tsar for loans and other help. This naturally increased the influence of the bureaucrats and gradually made of them indispensable supporters of the throne and of autocracy. In some instances the bureaucrat acquired thus even more power than the representatives of the oldest Russian families.

No wonder then that the bureaucratic career that could lead a man from the ranks up to the highest level of political life seemed attractive to so many Russian officials. But for autocracy and for the social system of the old régime it had a very serious drawback; it stood in contradiction to one of the most necessary principles of autocracy—the exclusiveness of the ruling class.

The Russian bureaucratic system never could develop such exclusiveness. The ranks of the government service were opened to any one. Personal ability and ambition could help any man to climb up the official ladder; and, as has been said, very many Russians availed themselves of these opportunities and actually did rise to the very top of the government system. But with them they brought into the system new ideas, broader views, personal hopes, thwarting and frustrating the class exclusiveness of the aristocrats. There necessarily came with them into the government system a more lively contact with Western Europe and with European ideas of government.

Many of those men could not stand for aristocratic exclusiveness; sometimes they even could not understand the psychology of aristocracy. In the end this was bound to undermine the communion between the aristocracy and the throne, because it created in the system so many purely personal interests. These interests soon became the source of a process of disintegration.

During the reign of Alexander III, these two groups still held and worked together, forming a solid foundation for the throne of the Tsars; but under the weak Nicholas II, the personal element soon began to dominate. The one group, aristocracy, was steadily losing power; the other one, the high bureaucracy, on the contrary, was gradually gaining influence and soon became the dominant force. If at that critical moment the leaders among the bureaucrats had established a firm contact with the other educated classes of more liberal principles and tendencies, for example with some of the groups of the Intelligentsia, the government might have undergone some changes and the system might have continued to exist a longer period of time. This could be accomplished, however, only on condition of acknowledging the necessity of participation in the government of new classes and social groups. But just this concession, bureaucracy was not willing to make. Most of the high officials did not want to share their privileges with outsiders and endeavored in many ways to exclude the intruders. This attitude of the higher bureaucracy explains the failures of the constitutional movement in the first decade of the twentieth century; bureaucracy decidedly defended autocracy.

Besides the two ruling groups just described, there was one more worth mentioning, the Court and the Family of the Tsar, though from the sociological point of view we find here still less cohesion and class feeling than in the bureaucracy. It was rather a group than a distinct class. Its social composition was constantly changing and fluctuating. There was a strong German element in this group too. The participation of the German element came from two sources, first, from the many marriages contracted by members of the Imperial Family with German princesses. There existed in Russia, as in many Western countries, the custom according to which members of the Imperial Family could marry only "equals," members of some other reigning house; and Germany was the only country where there were princess brides constantly available in excess. Secondly, from the times of Nicholas I, the Tsars, with the exception of Alexander III, had always a decided predilection for the Baltic Germans, whom they willingly appointed to the highest posts in the Empire and whom they often intrusted with the most delicate matters of government and administration. These Germans were usually better educated than their Russian colleagues, more experienced in the art of administration and stronger men individually; but above all, they were much more loyal to the principles of autocracy and to the Tsars, their masters. In the Baltic provinces, where these Germans were recruited, the local aristocracy was holding together much more effectively than in the Russian provinces.

This had, however, one unforeseen consequence;

these men kept somewhat apart from the rest of the government officials, rarely mixed with them and hardly ever accepted the purely Russian point of view in questions of government policies. They stood aloof from the Russians and formed a separate group in the Court surroundings. Perhaps just for that reason Court and government were never quite identical. This difference became very evident, especially in the reign of Nicholas II. On account of his weakness, personal influences became much stronger than previously; in the immediate surroundings of the Tsar a person close to him had always a better chance to exert individual influence.

Then, too, there was the Empress Alexandra, herself a German, with definite German tastes and prejudices, naturally preferring to deal with the Baltic Germans than with Russians, whom she never really understood and so often disliked.

With the Grand Dukes and the other members of the Imperial Family matters stood a little differently. In former days, up to the end of the reign of Alexander II, the Grand Dukes were very powerful and influential; many of them were active members of the government, some holding even ministerial positions. During the reign of Alexander III their powers were very much curtailed; nearly all of them were placed only in the military service, holding positions in the army or navy. In the time of Nicholas II further changes took place. At first some of the Grand Dukes still had high commands in the army; Alexis, for instance, was the nominal head of the navy. During the first years of the twentieth century, however, only a

few of them retained their positions and only exceptionally did they exercise any influence in politics.
There were two reasons for this. First, there arose
family troubles; the Empress did not like them and
the Tsar resented any advice or counsels, wherever
they came from. Furthermore, the family was rapidly
degenerating. Many morganatic marriages were taking place; in consequence some members were deprived
of their rights of succession to the throne; others were
exiled abroad or excluded from Court life and functions. Secondly, they themselves began to feel that
they were not popular with the people, who openly
resented their interference with politics. Notwithstanding the strict censorship, some papers succeeded
in making this resentment very clear; in consequence
the Grand Dukes preferred to retire to private life.
There were only two conspicuous exceptions: the first,
the Grand Duke Serge, uncle of the Tsar, whom the
latter appointed Governor-General of Moscow during
the most troublesome times. He made himself very
much hated by the radicals and liberals and was finally
murdered in February, 1905, by the revolutionaries.
The second exception was the Grand Duke Nicholas,
who commanded the Russian armies during the first
year of the Great War, but was peremptorily dismissed
in September, 1915.

Finally, we must mention the direct personal influences exerted by some very obnoxious individuals,
like the Frenchman Philippe and the disreputable Rasputin. The Tsar and his wife were always very sensitive
to mysticism and occult influences. They sought salvation and relief from their family and state troubles

and were constantly being fooled by such adventurers. These pernicious personal influences were naturally undermining the social basis of autocracy in the most effective way; they were, however, a product of the social decay that was developing in the ruling classes of Russia preceding the Revolution.

IV

The war with Japan was a severe test for the autocratic system, and it soon became evident that "the Russia that made possible an autocracy was hence quietly slipping away." * Since those fatal years of 1904–1905, Russia was gradually awakening from her century-long sleep; but such a process of awakening of 150,000,000 people could not develop silently and smoothly. Terrible shocks had to come, and the first signs of the storm became noticeable in 1905, when the defeat in Manchuria had thoroughly demoralized the Tsar's government.

A great wave of unrest swept over the country in 1905. During the summer months, especially after the disastrous battle of Tsusima, the liberals and progressives clamored for constitutional reforms quite openly. Several deputations were sent to Petrograd and received by the Tsar, who told them that he had promised a constitution and intended to carry out the promise. But instead, while the bureaucrats were discussing and debating, only curtailed reforms were being granted, culminating in the law of August, estab-

* Harold W. Williams, "Russia of the Russians" (Scribner's Sons, New York, 1914), **p. 49.**

lishing a consultative Duma instead of a parliament
wanted by the liberals.

As a direct consequence of this policy of hesitation
and half-measures came the labor movement of the
autumn of 1905, followed by railway and other strikes
that created great alarm both in the government
and in the nation. The liberals had lost the lead;
the movement was rapidly becoming radical and
nation-wide; revolution was knocking at the door of
autocracy.

Count Witte saved the situation for the moment,
having forced the Tsar to sign a manifesto granting
a real (though conservative) constitution and a bill of
rights.* After that the dissatisfaction rapidly subsided.

These acts of October 30, 1905, were juridically the
end of autocracy, though its political and social rôle
still lingered on for twelve years more. Unfortunately
we know at present that Witte had it in his power to
put an end to the old régime as well as to the former
legal system. Had he acted more resolutely and more
liberally, he could have given a start to a new constitutional régime that might have avoided for Russia
the sufferings of the Revolution. As it happened,
Witte's reforms only helped to prolong the agony of
the old régime and called forth a decade of political
contradictions very injurious to the country. The legal
system had already become constitutional, while the
social order remained still the old one. This is what
the Germans so characteristically nicknamed *Scheinkonstitutionalismus,* a sham constitutional régime, the

* Count Witte tells the story of the events of October, 1905, very
graphically in his "Memoirs," published in 1921 by Doubleday,
Page & Co., New York.

government constantly endeavoring to curtail it and hamper its development.

From the juridical point of view the acts of 1905 were, however, a constitution. The Tsar was no more the exclusive supreme power in the Russian State. There was created a new legal idea—the idea of law, which was hence to be not the expression of the will of a single individual (as hitherto), but an act arising from the coöperation of the Tsar and the two Houses of Parliament. No matter how the government struggled to reëstablish the exclusive authority of the Tsar, they could not succeed in ignoring entirely the coöperation of the Duma in legislation. They could do without the Duma by dissolving Parliament and often tried to govern the country by mere administrative decrees, but the constitutional principle still was there as a sad reminder of the promises of 1905.

Since then there has grown up a new and abundant literature of Russian constitutional law, previously unknown and at times even prohibited, expounding, strengthening and extending the principles of constitutionalism, against the wishes of the government, and effectively undermining the prestige of bureaucracy. The educated people began to realize the meaning of the political game that was going on in Petrograd. It can be summarized in the following way. The old social order, the ruling classes, did not want to accept the new constitutional ideas; and yet these ideas had come to stay. Maybe the cleverest among the reactionaries knew that their fight was hopeless, that it was only a question of time before constitutionalism would become finally established; but only the more bitter and ruthless became their actions. We can find numerous similar instances in the history of other nations.

This fight was conducted by both ruling classes in the same uncompromising spirit. The third element, mentioned above, the Court, the Imperial Family and the Tsar himself, played a much less independent rôle in this period. They were mostly used as mere tools to prolong the rule of the other two participants. Of the latter, aristocracy was fighting an entirely hopeless cause. This class was so evidently disintegrating that most Russians saw it. It was rapidly losing its social cohesion. It was being impoverished. It was degenerating. It was kept in power only by artificial means of government support. The aristocratic influence, in consequence, was more of the ideological type than the sociological; but they had only one idea in their defense that possessed any historical significance, namely, that they, the aristocrats and nobles, were the real social support of autocracy; the throne must begin to totter as soon as this class begins to weaken. Just this fact was being amply corroborated by the events of that period of Russian history.

The bureaucracy, on the other hand, seemed for a moment to have a better chance of prolonging its life. It controlled at the time the government machine, which looked still very powerful. The army was reformed and in much better condition. The police seemed strong and efficient. The spy system also appeared successful in working havoc among the revolutionary organizations. The nationalistic movement was being effectively crushed wherever it showed itself.

Stolypin, the exceptionally strong Prime Minister, was perfectly convinced of the efficiency of his government machine during the years 1906–1911. He sincerely hoped to save the régime; but in September, 1911, he was assassinated by his own agent. Only attentive observers could notice flaws in this showy display of strength.

In the very core of the system, however, there was a worm eating its way. It was a struggle for self-defense, but the bureaucracy itself was again by no means undivided in the fight. First, there were many bureaucrats who doubted both the purpose and the means used by the government; secondly, a steady process of demoralization set in, destroying the powers of the administrative machine from within. The first source of decay developed mainly because there were now many bureaucrats, even among the highest officials, who at the bottom of their hearts sympathized with liberal reforms and believed in human progress. These men, being themselves on the inside of the administration, saw its shortcomings. Their education made them realize that the Western systems of government were working far better than the Russian one, and that autocracy as a form of government was antiquated. In consequence, they could not give their services wholeheartedly. They had doubts and hesitations and never could agree to ruthlessness. They were always the first to suggest a compromise; but it was just those compromises, as we saw, that were so deadly for autocracy.

After 1905 the position of these men became really tragic. They were happy to accept the new consti-

Bureaucracy formidable yet divided over liberal constitution or conservative

tution, curtailed as it was, but soon realized that the
government was not taking it this way at all. The
policy of the Tsar and his ministers was to get back
to the old régime as much and as fast as possible. As
a result, these honest and sincere officials were faced
by a fearful dilemma, either to accept the policy or
to protest, which meant in the latter case not only
resignation or dismissal from office but giving the
people a new proof that public opinion was right in
blaming the government for its reactionary policy.
What better proof could there be that the administration did not conform with the idea of constitutionalism
than when its better elements resigned just on that
account! On the other hand, acceptance of the government's policy by these men forcibly meant a very immoral compromise, namely, the acquiescence with evil,
serving the mammon of unrighteousness and calling
forth a calamity upon their people. Such a state of
mind of the better officials could only further undermine the authority and strength of the government;
and as time went on it proved necessarily a potent
cause for the demoralization of the whole system.

Still worse was the case concerning the means used
by the government. They were doing much harm to
the nation. Even from the purely practical point of
view they were dangerous for the system. For example, these were the police measures of provocation
and the Russification of the non-Slavic peoples of the
Empire, the Imperialistic expansion in the Far East,
and the persecutions of the press for having criticized
the government. Many bureaucrats must have realized
the tremendous dangers of such shortsightedness; as

a matter of fact, many of them did vigorously protest. This again meant friction within the bureaucratic machine. No wonder that the machine could not work well any more.

No less potent were the forces of demoralization that developed in some branches of the administration. Worst of all in this respect was the decay of the police system. The "political police" and *gendarmerie* became quite independent, a sort of government within the government, very powerful, absolutely ruthless and without any scruples. Its ways of working were kept very secret; no investigation was ever allowed, no criticism tolerated, and any interference from without was strongly resented. Only once in a while, as in the case of Asef, the infamous agent of this system, was light thrown on its methods of work among the revolutionaries; but even then it was only a matter of chance that the corresponding story of Asef's deeds became known. Of course a system of government using such means could not last; it became only a question of time before it was bound to disintegrate.* As demoralization progressed, the political police acquired a frightful power over those who were serving the system, by simply enslaving them.

Exactly the same was happening, only perhaps in smaller proportions, in other branches of the Russian administration. The war ministry had its own scourge. The case of the War Minister, General Sukhomlinoff, is the best example. The administration of the non-Slavic provinces, too, was suffering from serious in-

* A glimpse into the methods of work of the police system is given by P. N. Miliukov in Chapter IV of his volume, "Russia and Its Crisis," Chicago University Press, 1905.

ward defects. There grew up, for instance, a whole class of men who made their living from the Russification of Poland, Finland or the Ukraine, who received promotion, decorations and high salaries for this kind of work, notwithstanding the fact that public opinion in Russia was against them, denouncing this foolish policy of the government.

Under these circumstances, the government and the system could not last. The granting of a constitution in 1905 was the death-knell of the régime. We saw how it was forced by the rising of national dissatisfaction, particularly during the unpopular war with Japan, to grant this important concession. One of the ministers, the late Krivosheïne, expressed this very well when, in one of his speeches, he mentioned the lack of understanding between "them" (the people) and "ourselves" (the ministers or the bureaucracy); "we" and "they" remained up to the Revolution as two distinct elements, like water and oil, never able to mix. With every year that passed, the cleavage between them tended only to increase until the final clash became inevitable.

Could that be avoided and how? This is the great historical question. The answer seems clear at present. Autocracy cannot compromise without perishing. As things developed in Russia between 1900 and 1917, the clash became absolutely unavoidable. The political system as well as the social order proved unable to adjust itself to new conditions of life. The hard crust of the Russian body-politic had, in consequence, to be broken up from within by the social forces bursting through. New political principles had to be established. The breaking up of the old régime was so very violent because first, it was artificially held back for a decade; and, secondly, on account of the great war that brought with it more terrible forces of demoralization and destruction. Thus the conflict became a national catastrophe of unheard-of dimensions.

It is quite another question how such a clash could have been avoided. Probably it could have been avoided, but only at the cost of the disappearance of autocracy; in other words, only on condition that the old régime would have honestly accepted in 1905 the end of autocracy and would have sincerely allowed the development of parliamentary legislation. Only on that condition could Russia have started on the path of liberal development and in time could she have acquired the necessary progressive institutions of a modern democracy.

Was that humanly possible? Could one expect the members of the old aristocracy and the Tsar's bureaucracy to give up of their own accord their privileges and ruling position? Hardly! Even among single individuals one does not often find such self-abnegation. For a whole class, and in this case for two classes simultaneously, such an effort would seem superhuman. At least nowhere in history do we find any such case of similar self-denial and sacrifice.

CHAPTER II

THE RUSSIAN PEASANT

I

THERE is one strange fact concerning the history of revolutions that has had no small influence on their valuation by our generation, namely, the little attention paid by even the most eminent historians to the attitude of the peasantry towards the revolutionary events. This is perhaps explained by the lack of brilliancy and by the very deeply laid roots of the social processes relating to the peasant class. Only recently did historians begin to analyze the social developments at all. Yet the rôle of the peasantry in most cases was of extreme importance. In France, as in Russia, for instance, the class of small farmers and tenants constituted the bulk of the nation and naturally formed the real background for the Revolution.

According to the teachings of some socialists, the French Revolution was called "political" because it brought to the front the middle class (the bourgeoisie) with its claims for political freedom and personal rights; the next great revolution (presumably the Russian one) was to be "social," admitting the labor class to power and based mainly on economic forces. The Russian Revolution effectively shattered that artificial theory. When the long expected events in Russia finally took place, it very soon became evident to attentive observers that this Revolution was just as "political" as the French one and disclosed, *pari passu,* the interplay of the same economic forces that acted in France in the eighteenth century. The only difference in this case was the appearance of a new social class as the ruling element in the state: Labor was ousting the bourgeoisie from power and striving to take the latter's place according to the old French proverb: *Ôtes-toi que je m'y mette.*

Such is the political meaning of both revolutions, French and Russian; the labor leaders naturally had different claims from those of the French bourgeoisie of the eighteenth century, but these were exactly of the same "political" nature as the bourgeois principles proclaimed in 1789. The "social" side of the Revolution of 1917, the Bolshevik experiment in communism, failed miserably. It produced only tremendous national suffering in Russia. As to the economic forces that led to the Revolution, they too were in both cases similar. They were fostering the awakening of a new class, making it conscious of the drawbacks of its situation and of its state of oppression, creating thus a claim for better treatment and for the equality of social opportunities.

But in both cases—and here we have the chief meaning of these revolutions—the social background and support for the revolutionary movements were provided by another class, the peasants, actuated by entirely different political motives and driven by other economic forces. Downtrodden and oppressed for centuries and always remaining in the shade, unorganized and uneducated, the peasants were the unconscious but enormously powerful social foundation over which the political and social readjustment was taking place. It was here, among the peasantry and making use of their economic dissatisfaction, that the revolutionary leaders were borrowing their strength and finding their support. In Russia, as in France, the peasants were still an inarticulate and dark mass, but in a state of blind fermentation, deeply dissatisfied and actuated chiefly by an intense land hunger that in both cases grew up historically from medieval times.*

In consequence, some of the most important developments that have taken place during the Russian Revolution cannot be understood nor interpreted in the right way without a previous attentive study of the history of the Russian peasants. It is this study alone that can give us the necessary explanations of many otherwise puzzling facts and developments.

II

The Russian peasant received his political freedom in 1861; for his economic advantages he is still fighting at present.

During the first half of the nineteenth century serfdom as a social institution was gradually deteriorating in Russia. On the one hand, education, contact with

* Comp. S. A. Korff, "The Peasants during the French and Russian Revolutions," *Journal of International Relations*, Vol. 12, No. 2, October, 1921.

the West, growing idealism, especially in literature and poetry, stimulated the best elements among the Russian people to fight serfdom in the name of liberty and humanity; on the other, changing economic conditions of trade, commerce and industry steadily lessened the economic advantages of the system of serf-labor. This necessarily deprived the ruling classes of the strongest stimulus for keeping it. The disasters of the Crimean war helped very much to convince the Russians that serfdom had lived its day and that a change was imminent and absolutely necessary. Many of the short-comings of the political system that brought about defeat could easily be traced to the institution of serfdom; the greatest evils of the social order could be attributed to that same cause.

A powerful wave of dissatisfaction swept the country as a result of the Crimean defeat; most of the conservatives and all of the liberals and progressives were clamoring in 1855–1856 for the emancipation of the serfs; the new Tsar, Alexander II, himself was convinced of the necessity of granting it. Only a very small group of "die-hards," composed of some of the richer landlords, aristocrats and nobles, of a few block-headed bureaucrats, and of a very small number of misled writers, were opposed to it.

Alexander promised the emancipation in several of his speeches; and, supported by a small number of enlightened statesmen, he honestly endeavored to work out the corresponding reform. But as time went on and the landowning nobility began to realize that emancipation meant certain loss of property and incomes to them, opposition to the reform began to grow among the ruling classes. The peasant serfs could not be emancipated without a certain amount of land being given them; they had to be provided with some means of existence, because their mode of living depended exclusively on the land they were tilling. The liberals who were working on the reform knew very well that a landless emancipation would mean a worse enslavement, and they were firm in their demand that land should be given the emancipated peasant. But where could this land be taken, if not from the former serf-owners? In other words, the landowning nobility realized that not only was it to lose the advantages of free labor (the serfs having always worked for the landowner without direct compensation), but, in addition, portions of its estates as well. Naturally opposition among the nobility and aristocracy became very strong. And as at the time the nobility was the ruling class *par excellence,* its opposition soon began to influence the Court and government. In taking advantage of the weakness of the Tsar, this group exerted upon him a tremendous pressure, endeavoring to thwart the reform.

This reactionary opposition did not succeed entirely in its objects, but did accomplish a very baneful curtailment of the proposed reforms, particularly in the most important question, that of landownership. The liberated peasants were not given sufficient land. Furthermore, though the amount of acres to be allotted to the peasants was determined by law, the landlord had the right to choose the location of the land to be given away and very often availed himself of this privilege to the detriment of the peasants; the latter received the worst lots, sometimes far distant from the village and most inconvenient for cultivation.

The average peasant allotment in 1861 was 6.21 acres; but as years passed and the population of rural Russia increased enormously in numbers, the peasant landholding per capita decreased to only 3.51 acres in 1900. The future prospect for the peasantry could be only further decrease and impoverishment.* No wonder that there developed among the peasants all over Russia a real Land-hunger.

One idea dominated of old in the psychology of the Russian peasant: "The work is my master's, but the land is my own." It originated in the dark days of serfdom as a sort of moral compensation and persisted to the Revolution as one of the most cherished hopes of the peasant. Its economic basis is a very natural one, the land being the source of life for the peasant. But unfortunately for him, the very same land was simultaneously a source of income for the nobleman who owned both the serfs and the land. Hence the conflict at the time of emancipation that ended unfavorably for the peasant and thus created a situation pregnant with terrific possibilities.

The decades that followed emancipation were a period of gradual increase of the primary evils of the peasant's life; the amount of land he held steadily decreased and the burden of taxation constantly increased. The peasant did not know how to increase the productivity of the land he tilled; he used very primitive methods, but could not improve the latter on ac-

---

* Comp., for example, P. Miliukov, "Russia and Its Crisis," Chap. VII; University of Chicago Press, 1905.

count of his lack of education. Then, too, for several
reasons he had no special stimulus to improve the land
culture (for instance, by the use of fertilizers). The
results of such possible improvements materialize only
after long years of waiting; but the peasant had no assurance that the land he tilled would remain in his
hands. He often believed that the advantages of his
improvements would be reaped by some one else, his
neighbor or his landlord. In consequence, he became
accustomed to rely exclusively on the natural productivity and richness of the soil, which, fortunately for
him, in most Russian provinces was very great. But
as soon as something unusual happened, a drought, an
epidemic, or epizoöty, it meant for him a genuine
catastrophe, which he was quite helpless to meet in
any way.

In most of the central provinces the peasants did
not own the land they tilled; usually they rented it
from absentee nobles or local magnates who were spend-
ing their lives far away in the cities, leaving the man-
agement of their estates to German or Lettish over-
seers. The peasants knew very well that in most cases
there existed no real bonds between the landlord and
his land except the law of ownership (which the peasants considered unjust); they realized that the nobility
was only exploiting the peasant-farmers and naturally
they resented it. The aristocracy, as well as the lower
gentry, always preferred government service to life in
the country; in the cities and in the service they found
an easier and much more pleasant life; and consequently only the poorest and most helpless among them
remained on their estates. Toward the end of the

nineteenth century there grew up a whole class of such impoverished gentry living in the country, but longing to join their wealthier relatives and friends in the towns.*

There was a moment in the reign of Alexander III when the government tried to develop by all sorts of means a policy of assistance to these impoverished nobles, but only to the detriment of the country, and without accomplishing anywhere marked results. The peasants knew it and naturally became convinced that they alone were right in claiming the whole of the land.

Of course in those days they could not ask for it openly; the government was much too strong for them, the police too vigilant, and the landlords too vindictive. At times only and in vastly separated localities did this feeling of dissatisfaction burst out, usually taking the form of ugly riots, easily quelled by the government. During the months that followed the defeats of the Japanese war these uprisings were at their worst. In certain localities they were very bloody; some landlords were killed and some mansions were burned.

This was the first warning of the peasants' attitude toward the landowning gentry. As we look back at it now, we see in the riots of 1905–1906 a convincing proof of the intense discontent of the peasant class. And the chief source of such a feeling was the land question. The peasants became firmly convinced that there existed a great injustice in the landowning system and that most, if not all, of the land ought to belong to them. During those years, while the liberal

* Many of the Russian novelists of the end of the century describe the tribulations of such poor noblemen. The most vivid pictures are given by Tchekhov.

middle class was fighting for constitutional reforms and personal freedom, the peasants were longing for one thing only. They wanted "more land"; not rented or otherwise limited real estate, but individual freehold, that they could dispose of at will. The ancient love of the peasantry for land was thus constantly being intensified.

Meanwhile, the government policy, with one exception, was in no way meeting the increasing difficulties of the situation. Instead of trying to satisfy the peasants, the government was using only force and coercion against them, patronizing and protecting only the ruling classes. The exception just mentioned was the law of November, 1906, which provided that the peasants could leave the village commune, purchase a patch of land, and own it in freehold. This reform was introduced by the Prime Minister, Stolypin, one of the few bureaucrats who had a clear idea of the dominant importance of the land question. He was counting on the political effects of individual freehold, knowing from lessons of history that the latter invariably proves to be one of the most conservative forces in politics.

In several provinces the reform of Stolypin did prove successful, satisfying the local Land-hunger of the peasants. But it had one serious drawback—the hasty manner of its enforcement. The government was so eager to introduce individual freehold that it did not hesitate to use all sorts of methods of coercion, doing thus more harm than good. For just that reason Stolypin lost the support of the educated people, the Intelligentsia; and without their assistance he could not succeed in allaying the peasants' dissatisfaction.

As a result, the reform did not lessen the distrust of
the peasants, who still continued to look askance at
the landowning gentry. Further, there arose opposition
from the latter, which at the same time created all
sorts of impediments for the government. It soon
became evident that the reform worked too slowly; its
benefits could not be apparent for some time to come.
Meanwhile the general dissatisfaction of the people
constantly increased, and educated classes combined
with the peasantry in blaming the government for the
growing economic evils.

III

There exists abroad a somewhat common misunderstanding concerning the Russian village commune, or
mir, as it is called in Russia. One often meets with
the assertion that the Soviet government originated
from just this institution and that in it can be found
the best promise for the future of Russia. Nothing
could be further from the truth, though even at present
many prominent socialists stake their hopes on the
mir.

One can find an excuse for foreigners having made
such a mistake in the fact that even the Russians
themselves for a long time misjudged its social and
political meaning. In the middle of the nineteenth
century, when Russian radicals and socialists were just
beginning to formulate their teachings, many men
among them firmly believed that the ancient *mir* was
a historical communistic institution. Only very few
socialists (the so-called "populists") denounced it as

reactionary; the reason for this latter assertion was that among the conservatives (for example, the so-called Slavophiles) there existed some who also glorified the *mir* as a source of possible salvation of Russia and the world. As a matter of fact, the Russian *mir* was and always remained a foremost weapon in the hands of the government, first, for assessing and levying taxes, and, secondly, for recruiting the army.*

The Russian government began to use the peasant commune for these two purposes in the sixteenth century. This was a period of great expansion; the Tsars were constantly conquering and colonizing new territories and were conducting endless wars with most of their neighbors. For such a policy of conquest they naturally needed two things—man-power and money. But as the administrative machine of Moscow of those days was still very primitive, weak and inefficient, those rulers could not effectively control the whole population and get out of it the much needed recruits and money. In order to obviate these difficulties, the Moscow government recurred to a very clever way of meeting them by making the whole village responsible for the payment of taxes and providing the army with the necessary recruits. Each village was assessed certain taxes and a certain number of recruits; how the villagers would distribute these burdens among themselves did not interest Moscow. This measure was also advantageous to the local landlords, who were obliged,

* Comp. P. Miliukov, "Russia and Its Crisis," Chap. VI (the author gives a detailed picture of the origins of the Russian commune); also M. Kovalevsky, "Modern Customs and Ancient Laws of Russia." Ilchester Lectures, Oxford, 1889–1890 (London, David Nutt, 1891).

on their part, to furnish recruits taken from among
their serfs; they, too, made the same use of the peasant
communes for assessing taxes. This fiscal object of
the *mir* remained in force for over two centuries and
began to lose its meaning only in the nineteenth century, when the government became much more
powerful and its administrative machinery more
efficient.

As soon as the government felt strong enough to be
able to dispense with the commune, the latter began
to deteriorate; but, of course, having existed for such
a very long period, it could not disappear at once.
Thus, the historical arguments concerning the inherent
love and predilections of Russian peasants for the *mir*
or their historical inability to live outside of it became
discredited; they were possible only so long as the
historians had not yet disclosed the secrets of the Russian Middle Ages.

There remained, however, a second group of arguments used mostly by ardent socialists. These latter
were willing to discard the question of the historical
origin of the *mir,* and were satisfied to assert that the
very long existence of this institution was sufficient to
explain the present-day communistic tastes and habits
of the Russian peasant, of which these socialists were
so firmly convinced. They did not care about the past,
but nevertheless built on this presumption their fondest hopes for the future. Their argument ran somewhat as follows: For many centuries the Russian
peasant was used to living in a commune; the latter,
in consequence, permeated the whole psychology of
the peasant, and shaped his economic views and ideas,

his conception of property and family life, and so forth. They argued that when the day of reforms came and they were able to approach the socialistic millennium, the peasant class, having always lived in communes, would acclaim such reforms and simultaneously provide a splendid social background for them. There was a good logical foundation for this argument if the peasant's psychology was really such as these theorists supposed; if it was, for historical or other reasons, communistic; and the historical facts seemed to tend strongly in that direction.

But just in this point those Russian sociologists and socialists were badly mistaken. They did not know and nobody could know at the time, least of all the peasants themselves, what the psychology of the peasantry would be in the matter after their political awakening had become an accomplished fact. The historical development does not always go along definite logical lines; these often come in sudden irrational processes or unexpected happenings that thwart the logical evolution of class feelings. The important fact to remember in this respect is that the peasants themselves were in no way conscious of these changes that were taking place. It was not only, as some people thought, simple ignorance of the peasants' life and ways of thinking on the part of the intellectuals, but an entirely new development in the peasant life, unforeseen by the teachers of socialism of the nineteenth century. During this century, as in preceding epochs, the peasants living under the communal system, the vast majority of them having previously been serfs, had not, and could not have, a clear idea of private property as applied to landownership; they had their personal belongings, but even then not always legally well guaranteed, on account of their precarious social status of inferiority and inequality. As to the land, in former days nothing belonged to them. After their emancipation in 1861, they did receive some, but, as was pointed out above, a very insufficient amount; in consequence, a desire for more land became predominant everywhere. But nobody could tell how the peasants would really feel when they should acquire finally the land they longed for. Formerly their feelings in this respect had been too abstract, too theoretical; this is what misled the theorists of socialism and allowed them to entertain mistaken hopes as to the future "peasant communism."

The socialistic writings, in turn, misled the foreigners, who studied the Russian situation and accepted these theoretical assertions for historical facts. Thus there originated the wrong theory of a connection existing between the Soviet government and the ancient peasant commune. It was only too natural for outsiders to believe the statement that the peasants were wholehearted communists and were willingly accepting the Bolshevik régime as a crowning of their longing for a communistic régime in general.

During the Revolution matters developed, however, on very different lines.

The first indications that the described theory of peasant communism was not corresponding to facts came in the early years of the new century. There already existed at that time many factors giving the peasants an opportunity to acquire real-estate property; and with them came signs of a new psychology of the peasantry, irrational and unexpected. In some provinces where better economic conditions prevailed there developed prosperity, and with it came savings and real-estate purchases by the richer peasants. But parallel to that there went on a process of gradual impoverishment of the gentry and of a steady withdrawal of the nobility from their estates. In many provinces the nobles were continuously selling their land, and much of it was being bought by the local peasants.* Yet these processes, though taking place all over Russia, were still deemed by the above-mentioned socialistic writers an exception, conditioned by special circumstances and in no way characteristic of the peasants' psychology in general.

Parallel to these processes of land acquisition by the peasantry, there developed some very unattractive traits in the peasants' character. Those among them who became rich and prosperous proved invariably very conservative and reactionary; only too often did they mercilessly exploit their peasant brethren; the Russians nicknamed them "Fists" (*Koolaki*) for their ruthlessness and cruel methods of coercion. But the most striking trait in this respect was their tenacious way of holding the property; once they succeeded in acquiring land they would not let it go under any condition.

More had to come, especially after the Japanese war, when Stolypin passed his land act of 1906. As was

---

* The two widely separated and in many ways very different provinces of Tambov and Samara (which the author knows personally, having lived there) had lost in the two decades of 1890–1910 more than two-thirds of their noble landlords, more than half of these estates having been sold to the peasants.

said, in some provinces the peasants availed themselves with pleasure of the possibility of "buying themselves out of the commune," notwithstanding the mentioned shortcomings of the law of 1906, of the government's faulty methods, and of the unpopularity of the act among the educated people. This time the indications of the growth of new ideas among the peasantry were much more serious. Some of the Russian economists pointed this out as an entirely new development standing in flagrant contradiction to the assertions and hopes of the socialistic writers. They rightly said that the exceptions to the general rule of "peasant communists" were becoming much too frequent and thus effectively undermining the very foundations of the socialistic theory; it seemed to these economists that the peasant, whenever he could get a chance, wanted and expected to acquire land in freehold, ridding himself of the communal system. "Give the peasant a chance," they asserted, "and he invariably will endeavor to hold the land in his own name, resenting and fighting any interference with his real-estate property."

Soon, however, there developed another sign, bringing with it an additional proof for the denial of the communistic theory. The conviction spread that the peasant *mir* was itself gradually decaying all over Russia, not only because of the desire of the peasants to acquire freehold but for other reasons too. In some provinces these new economic forces proved far more effective than the just-mentioned psychological factors. This is a very usual case in social processes.

In many localities the economic position of the peasantry gradually deteriorated. This was the case especially where the peasants had not sufficient land for cultivation. The small patches or strips of land they did have often changed hands; the land belonging to the village commune was periodically redistributed among the members of the commune; as a result, the latter had no incentive to improve their methods of cultivation, not only because of their own lack of education, but also because of the knowledge that in the near future they would lose it and the improvements they would have accomplished would profit their neighbors instead. The *mir* became itself a source of economic losses and disadvantages; and the peasants, shrewd as they always are, realized this very well. In other words, they began to blame the *mir* for their impoverishment and for the deterioration of agriculture in general. The economists, on their part, explained this as a very natural consequence of the communistic system; the village *mir* was precluding improvements by preventing and cutting out private initiative and by killing among the peasants any desire for amelioration. The most important point in the case is that the opposition to the *mir* was now coming from the peasants themselves and not from the bourgeois classes.

The practical result of all this was that during the years immediately preceding the Great War the *mir* had actually disappeared in some provinces, and though lingering on in others, was also evidently living its last days. It was moribund and was being undermined by the peasants themselves. Strange to say, there still remained theorists who were hoping against hope that this was only the consequence of the obnoxious political system or of the despised bourgeois social order. They staked their last hopes on a possible "social" revolution.

The Russian Revolution, however, shattered even these last hopes. In the summer of 1917, the Bolshevik leaders were preparing to seize the reins of power by upsetting the weak government of Kerensky; during their clever campaign they set forth, among others, the slogan of "Land," knowing very well how much the peasantry longed for land. "You want land?" the peasants were told. "Go and take it; who can prevent you?" And the peasants all over Russia did make a rush for the land; for many months there was going on everywhere, in consequence, stupendous land-grabbing, often accompanied by bloody vengeance, murders, incendiarism, and pillage.

There can no longer be any doubt that just this process of land-grabbing proved to be the strongest support and main source of strength of the Bolsheviki during the first year of their rule. The peasants were sincerely and devotedly backing the Bolshevik government in order to get the land they longed for; it was a tremendous and unconquerable social force, some ninety odd millions strong; and the Bolsheviki made good use of it, until a sudden disappointment destroyed their hopes and ruined their plans.

The Russian peasant was supporting the Bolshevik government in 1918 exclusively for practical purposes —for acquiring more land; and for a few months he felt content and satisfied. Then suddenly he realized that his hopes of landownership were vain, that the Bolshevik ideals and régime could not secure the hoped-for freehold. Bolshevism, as is well known, is communism, but communism denies private property in any form whatsoever. The peasants were told that, after all, the land they had acquired was not theirs, that it belonged to the commune, and not even to the village commune, but higher up—to the State. This seemed to them just as bad as the old régime of the Tsar and his gentry.

The Bolshevik government was never able to give the peasants any practical assurance that their new régime would last; on the contrary, the peasants clearly felt that since 1919 this régime was disintegrating and that it was an economic failure. Transportation broke down, money lost its value, industries died out and the city in consequence could not furnish the village anything it needed. Great dissatisfaction then began to spread among the peasants. They could not sell the surplus of their produce; money meant nothing to them because it no longer brought anything in exchange, the cities having nothing to give.

Further, when the peasants did have any surplus, in foodstuffs in particular, it was often taken away from them by force, by government requisitions. As a result, the peasants gradually stopped producing any surplus, limiting themselves to the strict minimum of their own family needs. This naturally was a great danger for the towns, as it tended to starve them, but the Bolsheviki were quite helpless; they could bring the horse to the trough, but could not make it drink; they could take away by requisitions what the peasant had, but could not force him to produce more.

Worst of all for the peasants, however, was another

matter, namely, the absence of any legal title to the
land they had acquired, the "scrap of paper" that gives
the citizen the positive assurance of ownership. After
having waited so long for the land, after having got
it at last, though often by foul means, the peasants
suddenly realized that they would not be able to keep
it and dispose of it freely in the future because the
new régime did not provide any legal right of property; and naturally they were frightfully disappointed.
But as soon as that happened and they stopped backing the Bolshevik government, the latter began to lose
its impetus and strength. It had no more the former
solid social background, and it gradually began to degenerate. The Bolsheviki tried to make concessions
and meet at least some of the demands of the peasants,
but all in vain; the gulf between them and the peasantry became constantly greater. They could not get
back the confidence of the peasants for the simple
reason that their foremost ideal, the communistic
denial of private property, was absolutely against the
grain of the peasants' conception of life. The peasant
was now heart and soul for private property; he intended to keep the land he had grabbed.* This was
the unexpected surprise that the Russian Revolution
had in store for those theorists who had fervently
hoped in former days that the historical development
of the peasant life in Russia would educate this class
to communistic ideals; they were so sure that the
peasantry were fond of the old *mir* and that in consequence it would be easy for them to accept the
Bolshevik communistic principles. As a matter of fact,

* Comp. *infra*. Chap. VI, Lessons of the Revolution.

things developed during the Revolution just the other way: the peasants did not realize in former days the meaning of private property as long as they did not possess any land. As soon as they got it, they meant to keep it; hence communism was doomed. The peasant in this respect became more bourgeois than the educated people of the middle classes. Maybe this is the hopeful factor that will produce in future Russia a stable government. There are signs, though, that another surprise and disappointment may be in store for the coming generations; the Russian peasant may become a very conservative and reactionary force in politics.

IV

In the foregoing gloomy picture there is, however, one hopeful sign for the future. Under the impulse of the Revolution the peasants are awakening very fast from their centuries of slumber. Revolution itself is a mighty factor in this respect and achieves its results remarkably quickly. And with the awakening come new ideas and a desire for better government, an intenser realization of what government and administration mean and of how they affect local life. To the peasant there came simultaneously the realization that he himself was rather helpless on account of his lack of education. He saw that he could not achieve anything without leadership and began to see that leadership could come only from the educated class, the Intelligentsia; and, on the whole, he became willing to accept that leadership. Though there still lingers in some cases a certain distrust of educated men, which has grown up on account of the past historical conditions of peasant life, or simply because the educated men are not "their" men, yet one can easily detect at present many cheerful signs of the willingness of the peasants to accept such leadership. This alone can achieve the desired end of establishing in Russia a sound and democratic form of government.

The educated people, on their part, are quite ready to coöperate in this respect. They have learned the lesson from the Revolution that the peasants really constitute the Russian nation; being in such a vast majority—nearly eighty-five per cent of the population—their interests must forcibly dominate in future Russia and influence the policies of the coming government.

The devotion of the educated Russians to the cause of liberalism and cultural progress was sufficiently demonstrated long ago during the protracted fight with autocracy. Already at that period the young men and women were ready to make any sacrifice, willingly giving up their own lives for the freedom and liberty of their country. And there is not the slightest proof that this has abated in the least in our day.

In this respect a most prominent rôle in the past has been played by the zemstvos, or local self-governing units, which always attracted the best elements from among the educated people. There is very good reason to believe that in the future these same local self-governing organizations will again take an important part in the regeneration of Russia. The Russian liberal and constitutional movement historically centered in the zemstvos; the latter gave Russia the best generation of statesmen the country ever had; we are still proud of them, especially of the first generation among them during the sixties of the last century.

The zemstvos, as a system of local self-government, were established in 1864. This was one of the most important concessions to public opinion made by the government of Alexander II. It was a consequence, first, of the Crimean disaster that so vividly disclosed Russia's internal weakness, and, secondly, of the emancipation of the serfs, that necessitated a revision of the whole system of provincial administration.

The government of Alexander II intended originally to hand over to the zemstvos the whole local administration of the provinces; but as reaction set in, the zemstvos were gradually deprived of some of their most important functions which the government turned over to the provincial governors and police agents.

The zemstvos were organized in the following way: Each district (corresponding somewhat to the American county) and each province had its own zemstvo, consisting of an assembly and an executive council. The zemstvo assemblies of the districts and provinces met regularly once in three years and elected the executive officers, made up the yearly budget, and discussed local affairs, though always under the strict supervision of the governors. Suffrage was limited, mostly by landownership; in consequence, the landlords dominated in many provinces, but not the richest among them; it was the middle class, the local gentry, that played the most important rôle. Peasant delegates often participated, but never wielded any influence

worth mentioning. The executive power was in the
hands of a council, or *ooprava,* elected for three years
and responsible to the local assembly, but also under
the supervision of the governor. The chairman of the
ooprava was usually entrusted with the most important and difficult tasks.

As time went on and reaction became stronger, the
control of the governors over the zemstvos became constantly more rigid; in many cases the governors interfered with and frustrated the work of the zemstvos.
The governors were appointed by the Tsar and wielded
wide powers in the provincial administration; they
were responsible only to the central government, but
as publicity did not exist during the old régime, their
responsibility was practically nominal; their misdeeds
and mistakes were hardly ever disclosed or tried in
courts; the government always endeavored to hush up
the cases when the authority of the governors was
questioned. This is the most usual evil of any bureaucratic system; in Russia it was especially the case, as
there developed a certain *esprit de corps* among the
government servants.

Not content with the described powers of supervision
over the zemstvos, the government of Alexander III
in the eighties introduced one more offensive reform.
It passed a law in 1889 introducing a new form of local
government that further curtailed the functions of the
zemstvos. Special officers were appointed, having
simultaneously administrative, police and judiciary
powers. The mixing up of the police and judiciary
powers very soon proved most obnoxious. These new
officials, called *Zemskii Nachalniki,* were selected ex-

clusively from among the local gentry. And here we have the explanation of the real object of this reform; the government endeavored by these artificial means to support the degenerating nobility. The government was cognizant of the many signs that pointed to the steady decay that was setting in among that ruling class; but Alexander's ministers were hoping to stop or at least delay this process as much as possible by securing for the local gentry a dominant position in the system of provincial administration.

This unfortunate reform proved, however, extremely dangerous for the nobles themselves, as they soon lost, in consequence, their last prestige among the educated people and made themselves wholeheartedly disliked by the peasantry. The main principle of this reform, making a judge of a police officer and often in cases in which he was personally interested, was a terrible mistake and stood in flagrant contradiction to the theory of separation of powers of administration and judiciary. Possibly these evils could be somewhat mitigated by enlightened influences of educated jurists, but as the reform was so very unpopular from the very beginning, the best and educated Russians shunned this sort of work. The government soon found itself forced, in consequence, to appoint to the new positions the first-comers and applicants, without being able to make any selection of better men. As a result, most of these officials were taken from among the least educated gentry, which naturally could not lead to any improvement in local administration. On the contrary, rather, the zemstvos distinctly suffered from the interference of these officials in questions of self-government; and as these men usually had the backing of the governor, they could achieve the objects of their interference very easily and usually to the detriment of the zemstvos.

Not only did the educated people look askance at the *Zemskii Nachalniki,* but the peasants also feared and despised them, resenting their personal rule as a remnant of the former dominance of the noble land-lords and serf-owners. These officials had naturally most to do with the peasants in the local administration; they were always in very close contact with them, being the local judges and administrators of peasant affairs nearly everywhere. The peasants thus came to consider them the typical representatives of autocracy and of the ruling classes.

On account of their lack of education and very primitive ways of administering justice, the *Zemskii Nachalniki* must have seemed to the peasants very crude types of administrators. This naturally was bound to strengthen the class feelings of the peasants already existing against the nobility in general. What could the peasants expect from the ruling class except selfish oppression?

In consequence of these numerous causes of inefficient administration, class egotism, land-hunger, and mutual distrust, there gradually grew up an impassable chasm between the peasants or the mass of the people, on the one hand, and the local gentry and nobility, feared and disliked by the former, on the other.

When revolution came, these ill feelings of the peasantry burst out in a frenzy of vengeance against the nobility at large; the nobles paid dearly for the mistakes of autocracy and were doomed to evaporate and vanish as a social class from present-day Russia. The peasant masses came to hold their own and are now firmly established as a political force of the future. Salvation lies, as was pointed out above, in the willingness of these masses to accept the leadership of the progressive and educated Intelligentsia.

CHAPTER III

THE RUSSO-JAPANESE WAR

I

In the historical appreciation of the Russian Revolution, the Russo-Japanese War plays an important rôle. It was this war that called forth the first revolutionary events, when all over Russia dark political clouds were already gathering and the revolutionary thunder was distinctly heard in some quarters. Later on the social dissatisfaction abated somewhat, the local uprisings being successfully quelled by the government; but as we look back at them now, we can easily see that in miniature they had exactly the same characteristics as the events of the Revolution of 1917. Less intense, without much coördination or interdependence, they were not sufficiently appreciated by contemporaries. Many people did not realize in 1905 the full meaning of the movement and that it was a proof that autocracy had entered the final stage of its existence.

The historical meaning of this war can be summarized in the following way: it was the start of the social movement, the people rebelling against the existing political system of government. The war actually brought with it the legal end of autocracy, a

mild constitutional reform having been introduced in
October, 1905. From this month on we can witness the
last period of the social struggle of the old régime, endeavoring by force and coercion to prolong its life
artificially.

The Russo-Japanese War can be studied from three
points of view; namely, first from the point of view of
political and diplomatic history, which would comprise
the analysis of the events that brought about the war,
its causes and origins; secondly, from the military
point of view, which would mean the study of war and
peace, of the military events, the conduct of the war,
the effects of the defeat, the failures of Russian military
leadership and the conclusion of the Portsmouth Peace;
and, thirdly, from the point of view of consequences of
the war, of what it brought about in Russia and how
the social discontent grew in proportions and strength
during the last years of autocracy.

The causes and origin of this unfortunate war are
well known at present. They all point one way: it
was a foolish and shortsighted experiment in imperialism, extremely dangerous for the existing political
order and absolutely of no advantage to the Russian
people. The government was blind to the dangers of
this enterprise on account of the guiding principles of
the autocratic régime and also because of "friendly"
urgings and counsels of Russia's western neighbor, playing his own game.

The history of Russia's foreign relations for the preceding century clearly shows that all her interests and
all her former policies tended strongly westward and
southwestward. This was also the direction of her

economic expansion and the goal of her political
ideology. Here in the west were the warm seas, the
best markets for Russian raw materials; here was also
the greatest need of Russian help, in her foodstuffs or
oil, timber or minerals. The economic and political
meaning of Russia's exports westward can well be appreciated at present, since Russia is eliminated from
European markets. Her growing industries in the
latter part of the nineteenth century were entirely dependent on Western markets as well as on Western
capital.

Then suddenly, as though moved by some powerful
evil influence, Russia turned eastward and started on
her fatal imperialistic adventure in the Far East,
thousands of miles distant from her economic and
social center, in a country very sparsely populated and
having in view the exploitation of lands and regions
where just at that time another very powerful and
dangerous neighbor was also endeavoring to expand.

For this reason a clash became sooner or later unavoidable. Had Russia contented herself with her
natural eastern boundaries along the northern shores
of the Amur river and with the rich hinterland of
Yakutsk and Kamchatka, the dangerous encounter
with Japan might have been avoided. The Russian
government, however, meant to move southward into
Manchuria and China, encroaching even on Korea,
where the Japanese were already deploying their
forces.

The first threatening signs of Russian expansion
in the Far East became evident during the Sino-
Japanese War. Russia was not only energetically back-

ing Li-Hung-Chang at the time of the Shimonoseki peace transactions, but was getting ready for an active interference in the Far Eastern trouble. Moreover, Russia was not alone in the game; France was supporting her by promising financial assistance, while England and Germany were also endeavoring to get a share in the division of spoils.

First came the money loans to China with all sorts of political conditions attached to them; then the exploitation of Chinese markets, the building of railroads and finally the so-called "leases" of territory. All this came very near to the partition of the Chinese Empire. In most instances Russia was playing the leading part.

After the Shimonoseki Peace was signed, Russia with the other great Powers forced Japan to return Port Arthur to China, but only in order to take this harbor a few months later herself. The Russians occupied Port Arthur and the Germans took Kiaochow in March, 1898.* A little later England took possession of Wei-hai-Wei and France of Kwangchowwan. Japan very naturally felt hurt and was bound sooner or later to avenge herself. At that time she was yet too weak and isolated to be able to protest and withstand the pressure of the Great Powers; she had to bide her time and first try to find a friend and ally.

There exist many indications that at first Japan would not have been averse to a friendly understanding with Russia, delineating in the Far East the mutual interests of these two countries. It would have been

* For further details see S. A. Korff, "Russia's Foreign Relations during the Last Half Century"; Macmillan, 1922.

only natural; the two countries were close neighbors, interested in the same matters, very similar as to their political systems of government, and both intent on imperialistic expansion. They could have easily come to terms and divided amicably their spheres of influence in China, Manchuria and Korea. But from the very beginning the Japanese met only haughtiness and an overbearing unfriendliness on the part of Russia. For this reason no cordial understanding was possible. The Russians repeatedly refused to consider the Japanese as their equals and ruthlessly insisted on their own extreme claims. There were also marked personal elements in the demeanor of the Russian government. The Tsar and some members of his family had invested money in Korean concessions, mostly along the Yalu River. This was forcing the Russian expansion still further south into Korea.

Expecting a conflict, Japan began to arm and get ready for it, while the Russians, in their haughty attitude, were complacently neglecting the many political warnings and taking no preparatory measures whatever. In the diplomatic transactions that followed they adopted the method of procrastination and systematically refused to give Japan clear and concise answers. Japan finally lost patience and presented her last demands in a note that amounted to an ultimatum; not getting any definite reply even then, she started the war by attacking the unprepared and undefended Russian squadron at Port Arthur on a dark February night of 1904.

If we keep in mind the policies of both countries before the war, we can easily discern the potent causes that led them to this dangerous conflict. On the part of Japan, it was her ambition not only to become a dominant factor in the Far East, but to enter the Comity of Nations and become a Great Power. In other words, she wanted to enter the inner circle of the ruling Powers of the world. Great Britain, very much fearing Russia at that time, was energetically helping the Japanese to strengthen their international prestige.

Japan had set her heart on exploiting Korea and the South Manchurian markets. She needed both of them for their raw materials and for selling there her own industrial products. But politically there existed other motives also; namely, in the dominance of a military caste with very warlike and imperialistic ideals, in the autocratic form of government and in the lingering resentment against Russia for having thwarted the Japanese aims in 1895. The seizure of Port Arthur was particularly resented by Japan; and the haughty treatment the Japanese received at the hands of the Russian bureaucrats was another psychological factor motivating her policies. One must remember, finally, the ambition of the Japanese government to become a Great Power and the overwhelming dread she had of the Russian aggression in the Far East.

On the part of Russia, the causes that brought on the disastrous war with Japan were somewhat different. The outward motives were evident long ago; but behind them there existed also hidden potent social causes. The outward motives can be summed up in two words: imperialistic expansion. This expansion had two very characteristic traits; first, it was a case of pure imperialism, and, secondly, it was absolutely contrary to Russia's historical development and to her best interests. This policy was started and conducted by a small group of government officials with the support of the Tsar himself, and had for its object personal advantages. Some of the instigators were seeking fame, others power and distinction, still others personal influences or pecuniary advantages, but none of them were considering the interests of the nation. Count S. J. Witte was the single conspicuous exception; he certainly did consider the interests of Russia, though he started a very dangerous policy and by 1902 must have realized the peril. He had hoped to acquire in the Far East new markets for the growing Russian industries and also to establish an outlet for Russian exports to the warm waters of the Pacific. The danger of his policy, though essentially peaceful, lay in the fact that it provided a great temptation for the militaristic and imperialistic elements to tamper with it and to make use of it. As a matter of fact, these elements among the Russian government very soon did interfere with Witte's policy and were bound to acquire a dominant influence. When Witte saw this, it was too late; the Russian government was running fast toward disaster; his warnings could no longer stop it.

The more important social forces back of these purely personal motives can be summarized in the following way. Autocracy no longer felt as strong as in former days; there existed many factors, as we saw in the preceding chapters, that effectively undermined its strength. Feeling this, the ruling classes, and especially the bureaucracy, were trying to find new fields of action. Imperialistic expansion in such cases often seems very tempting; it can bring with it, if successful, pecuniary advantages and thus furnish some vital assistance to the ruling classes; it can provide them in case of success with new incomes and more glory and give them a new lease of life. These possibilities attract especially the bureaucratic elements of the ruling classes; there is in such cases a distinct feeling of adventure.

During the latter part of the nineteenth century, when bureaucracy became in Russia more powerful than ever and when many men were rising to high offices from the lower ranks of the people, this idea of an adventurous experiment in the Far East, conducted in distant lands, the nation not really knowing nor understanding what was going on there, seemed alluring and tempting to many bureaucrats. Some officials even hoped to be able to make use of it at home in order to cope with the revolutionary movement in a more efficient way; as long as there were exciting things going on in Siberia and China, the nation's attention, they thought, might be distracted from the social evils. But this proved to be a mere gamble, and those bureaucrats and adventurers who staked their hopes on it, had soon to realize their frightful mistake. Instead of satisfying the people and quieting the discontent at home, they aroused, on the contrary, only worse hatred and dissatisfaction; and a few of them paid dearly for it. The heaviest loser, however, was Russia herself.

In other words, the policies that started the dangerous Far Eastern expansion were a pathological product of the autocratic régime of Russia; the country had no longer a healthy government ruling it. Outwardly still very powerful, a seeming military colossus, Russia was internally handicapped by a very inefficient political system that had lost its contact with the nation; it was no longer responding to the needs and interests of the people, being driven and actuated exclusively by the selfish interests of small ruling classes.

II

How little Russia was prepared for war became evident from the very first days of the struggle with Japan. When it came to the practical test of the Russian military strength, Russia's forces gave way in nearly every respect and every case. This was due not to any lack of personal courage or to any individual cowardice; on the contrary, the Russians, officers and soldiers, fought as valiantly as ever, going through terrible hardships and sacrificing their lives willingly, though the people at large never really understood the meaning of the war. The reverses were due mostly, if not entirely, to the defects of the system of government, to its frightful inefficiency, and to its unpopularity among the educated people.

This was probably the most important lesson of the war; autocracy might have learned it, but did not. A serious war with a strong and determined opponent cannot be fought without the wholehearted support of the nation. But on account of the shortcomings of autocracy it was just that support that was lacking from the beginning of the hostilities. With the exception, perhaps, of the very first weeks of the war, when a certain enthusiasm seemed to have flared up, kindled mostly by the unexpected attack of the Japanese on the Russian fleet at Port Arthur, the nation at large did not understand the meaning of the war, did not know its objects and hardly admitted any justification for it. This is so very evident if one compares Russia's case with that of Japan! In Japan every citizen knew what his country was fighting for; every Japanese realized that the whole future of his country was at stake. Japan also was an autocracy, her system of government also was by no means democratic, though it had been very much modernized during the decade preceding the war and had made strenuous efforts to cast off its antiquated medieval aspects. The Japanese policy was very militaristic and imperialistic, intent on an economic expansion. But there was that one great difference—the ruling classes in Japan were in very close contact with their nation; they knew how to explain the situation to the people and how to convince them of the reality of the Russian danger; they made use of the foolish aggressiveness of the Russian government, for which, as we saw, there was no excuse. The Japanese cleverly spread the notion, among their people as well as abroad, that they were fighting against a deadly national danger. In many countries, including the United States, the sympathies were on Japan's side; she was thought to be the sufferer of Russian aggression; and in Japan every citizen was ready to do his duty and to support his government. In consequence, although much inferior in military strength and economic resources, Japan still was winning all along the line.

This fact stands out very clearly in the memoirs of General Kuropatkin,* who was for a time the Commander in Chief of the Russian armies in Manchuria. But just these same memoirs are a strong indictment of the Russian government, and there is little wonder that the Tsar ordered their suppression. Take, for example, the inefficiency of the commanding generals on the Russian side. Very few of them showed any military skill; most of them were ignorant, quarrelsome, conceited and selfish. Kuropatkin bitterly complains of this and repeatedly blames the central government for having sent him such men to fight the Japanese. But whose fault was it, after all, that these men had high commands at home? Most of them were promoted and appointed by this same Kuropatkin while he was Minister of War and only in consideration of court influences and "pull." Kuropatkin himself was a very typical representative of that régime. Thus while conducting the war, Kuropatkin for a long time underestimated the strength of his opponents, which is always a great mistake for a military commander; secondly, he constantly kept an eye on St. Petersburg, the capital, carefully watching the court intrigues, the Tsar's demeanor and the bureaucracy's doings; when some ignorant general was appointed to a high command by the home office or when a man was trying to interfere with Kuropatkin's own actions, the Commander in Chief rarely had enough courage to protest with the Tsar. As a necessary result, the whole campaign was bungled and the war was finally lost.

* "The Russian Army and the Japanese War," John Murray, London, 1909.

It was the direct and unavoidable outcome of the methods of autocratic government. The whole war was like a mirror in which one could plainly see the defects of the Russian government system. The technical inefficiency and disorganization, the ignorant personnel, the incompetent generals and the weak Commander in Chief himself were all the consequence of the régime.

One must say, however, that many educated Russians realized this nearly from the beginning of the war. As they could not be sympathetic to the aims of the war they took a strong pacifist attitude. The more radical the political parties and organizations were, the more definitely they protested against the war in general. Gradually there grew up among the Russian socialists and radicals a conviction that the military defeat could even be useful for Russia in disclosing the defects of autocracy, in demoralizing the government and in helping to bring about constitutional reforms.

Toward the end of the war, especially in the summer of 1905, those feelings became very strong indeed and helped very much the spread of general dissatisfaction among the nation. The government naturally was helpless, becoming speedily disorganized and demoralized. This necessarily influenced the morale of the army and effectively undermined its powers of resistance. Consequently, toward the end of the summer, peace was already in sight. There lingers, however, in the minds of many Russians even at present, the conviction that peace with Japan in 1905 came too early, that it would have been much better for many reasons to have deferred the peace transactions. There are two points of view in this respect, very different in their appreciation of the political situation of 1905.

One group, to which belonged many old generals and conservatives, Kuropatkin himself included, was still hoping for victory; their main argument was that in September, 1905, Russia was stronger than ever before; their proofs were almost entirely strategic and statistical, showing the increase in strength and numbers of the Manchurian army. But at present one can doubt their statements, because, as they said themselves, the morale of the army was steadily degenerating.* The point of view of the second group is very different, and their arguments seem very convincing even at the present day. They believed that Russian victory was out of the question, because of the lack of support of the war by the nation; but according to them, had the war lasted a few months longer, the Tsar's government would have further disintegrated and a stable constitutionalism would have been the necessary outcome. Constitutional reforms were granted in October, 1905, but the old régime, being still strong, soon recovered and started to retract the constitutional promises of 1905. This flare-back of autocracy would not have been possible, these men maintain, had the government been more effectively undermined by a few more months of war. On the other hand, all the evidence we possess tends to show that Japan was also at the end of her tether, that her economic resources were giving out and that she could

* Comp. Kuropatkin's "Memoirs," Vol. II, chapters on the Causes of the Russian Defeat.

not have kept on fighting much longer. This would have meant a military draw, but politically it would have brought about a period of constitutional reforms in Japan also. The lack of any definite success would have undermined necessarily the prestige and authority of the Japanese military and imperialistic ruling class. In other words, had the war lasted a little longer, it would have called forth a democratization of Japan. And after all, the fate of the Far East always depended on that most important fact. Imperialism there cannot be either effectively fought or stamped out until Japan herself becomes a democracy.*

The Portsmouth Treaty was a diplomatic victory for Russia and for her clever plenipotentiary, Count Witte. Russia came out of the war with very few territorial losses and without having to pay any war indemnity at all; she lost only half of the Island of Sakhalin. But morally she was defeated, humiliated and prostrate. The meaning of this defeat was evident not so much in the East as in the West. In order to appreciate this sad consequence we have to analyze another element of the diplomatic history of that epoch, namely, the rôle played by Russia's western neighbor.

III

During the first decade of the twentieth century, while Russian imperialism was at its worst, Berlin was playing a very shrewd and clever game. The plan of the German government was to involve Russia as much

* Shortly after the war there was written a very interesting book by a Frenchman who sized up very well the Russian situation; see A. Chéradame, "Le Monde et la Guerre Russo-Japonaise," Paris, Librairie Plon, 1906.

as possible in Far Eastern affairs; by advice, intrigue, personal influences, flattery and deceit, the Germans were urging the Russians to commit themselves to Far Eastern aggression. The Kaiser was whispering in the ear of the Tsar all sorts of evil counsels, sometimes threatening, sometimes flattering him. There exist many proofs of this nefarious influence of Germany. We know now that it was a carefully planned and systematic game that she was playing, the object being to involve Russia so much in the Far Eastern troubles that she would become weak or even powerless in the West. The Germans knew very well that the existing régime of Russia was so inefficient that it could not cope with the increasing difficulties either at home or abroad and that the new troubles with Japan were bound to be disastrous and to take all of Russia's strength, thus eliminating her influences from European affairs. That is just what Germany wanted. It really meant the effective neutralization of the Franco-Russian Alliance, leaving France once more face to face with Germany, but with a Germany that was steadily increasing her powers, becoming daily more dangerous and more threatening. Not having any strong opponent on her eastern frontier after the breakdown of Russia, Germany rightly expected to have a free hand in the west. And one must acknowledge at present that after the Japanese War was fought and Russia defeated and humiliated, Germany did score a great success; for a moment she seemed to have attained her ambitions of glory and might. This situation must always be kept clearly in mind for the impartial study of the origins of the Great War of 1914.

Meanwhile, very grave political and social events developed in Russia as a consequence of the Japanese War.

During the summer of 1905 protests, manifestations and meetings were taking place everywhere; and the people were trying to force the Tsar to grant constitutional reforms. For a third time in the history of Russia * a very important rôle was played by the zemstvo organizations. During the Japanese struggle they had been united into one union for war purposes. The zemstvos were helping the Red Cross to care for the wounded and prisoners of war; they were also assisting the government in furnishing supplies to the army in Manchuria. This unification increased appreciably the strength of the zemstvos and encouraged them to continue their political fight. It is out of that organization that the Constitutional-Democratic party, usually called the Cadet party, grew up; it was the zemstvo political program that became the foundation of the constitutional claims of the Cadets.

In August, however, came a new disappointment; instead of granting the long expected parliamentary institutions, the government announced the establishment of a consultative Duma; a body, though elected by the people on the basis of rather broad suffrage principles, yet having no real legislative authority. This proved a terrible shock for the nation; most citizens realized then that autocracy was not willing to

* The first two occasions when the zemstvos played such an important rôle were: first, in the seventies, when self-government was being effectively introduced in Russia; and secondly, in the nineties, when the zemstvos tried to persuade Nicholas II to grant reforms on the occasion of his accession to the throne.

give in and that, in consequence, there was bound to be a political fight. Dissatisfaction burst forth everywhere; strikes, riots, uprisings followed, the government gradually becoming absolutely demoralized.

It is interesting and important to compare these events of the autumn of 1905 with the Revolution of 1917. We see exactly the same developments in both cases, with only the difference that in 1905 their scope was much more limited. Their essence, their principles and moving power were absolutely identical; the same motives were apparent, the same forces were displayed, but in miniature, on a reduced scale, of much smaller dimensions. Comparing them, we easily see the striking similarity of both processes.

There is an interesting conclusion that can be drawn as to the meaning of historical lessons in general. Had people realized the essential motive powers driving the nation in 1905 to vent its dissatisfaction, many evil consequences and much suffering could have been avoided. At the time, in 1905, these evils were not yet strongly developed; one could easily cope with many of them; one could at least prevent their further increase; there was ample time for such preventive action. The best examples in this case are the land-hunger of the peasants, that became so evident in their attacks on the property of the landed nobility, and the "constitutional" hunger of the Intelligentsia, clamoring for constitutional reforms and for the participation of the nation in legislation and government.

The fault of not heeding these many warnings lay with the ruling classes and the government that represented these classes. Concessions were finally made, but each time under terrible pressure and very insincerely and with the animus or intention of withdrawing them as soon as circumstances would permit. Of the weak Tsar, the Court and the reactionaries nothing else perhaps could have been expected. They saw the danger, they knew what was coming to them in case of a constitutional change, and realized that it would mean the loss of power and of all their former privileges and advantages. The liberal literature and the protests of the progressive parties and organizations made this very clear and discussed such possibilities in full detail. No censorship was able any more to force them to be silent; the government could no longer sufficiently control the situation. There exists in consequence an explanation, if not an excuse, for the actions and policies of the reactionaries. They knew very well that it was a death-struggle for *their* régime.

Not so with a few outstanding bureaucrats whom chance had brought to the front of political events during those fatal months. They could have helped in bringing about a change to constitutionalism that would have saved much suffering for Russia. And the main blame in this case falls upon Count Witte who had the best chance of all. He had then just returned from Portsmouth and had told the Tsar the whole truth about the political situation in Russia in his usual blunt way; he pointed out that if a constitution were not granted at once, a revolution would unavoidably take place. The general strike, then proclaimed, seemed to amply justify his warnings. The Tsar hesitated for a few days but finally was forced to give in.

After that, it was only natural that the reform

should be intrusted to Witte. He had the initiative, he seemed to have a plan of action, he sized up the situation at the most critical moment, he had wide relations abroad, and finally, he had among reactionaries the reputation of a liberal; at least the Tsar certainly thought him to be a liberal. And that is just where they were badly mistaken and why Witte failed in the great task intrusted to him.

He did work out a constitution and had a bill of rights attached to it, forcing the Tsar to sign both acts on October 30, 1905. As a first step toward constitutionalism these two acts were certainly good enough. Had they been carried out sincerely and honestly, they no doubt would have satisfied the Russian nation very well. But it was just in this last respect that serious trouble soon developed; they were not carried out in an honest way, and as we know at present, could not have been thus carried out on account of Witte's own shortcomings.

On the same day, October 30, 1905, Witte was appointed Russia's first Prime Minister. In former days there was no Prime Minister in Russia because the Tsar was legally held to be the exclusive head of the administration, all the ministers being juridically equal and strictly subordinated to the Tsar; it was from him only that the direction of policies emanated. This naturally had to change with the introduction of constitutional principles; the government had to be consolidated, unified and intrusted to one head, a Prime Minister, the executive power having been at last separated from the legislative one.

Having received this coveted appointment, Witte

proceeded to build up a new government on the cabinet system. It was at that moment that his difficulties began. He arranged for several conferences with prominent liberals, such as Miliukov, Prince Lvov, Prince Trubetzkoi, Shipov, Kovalevski. He spoke to them singly and in groups and from the very start received invariably one and the same reply: they would be willing to coöperate with him and accept ministerial portfolios only on the absolute condition that the new government would take a definite constitutional stand and would be allowed to carry out the promised constitutional principles, establishing a régime of personal freedom. This meant, however, making a clean sweep of the old régime, and just this Witte was not willing to do. For him personally it would have meant a definite rupture with the Tsar, the Court, and the reactionary elements behind the scenes. From his own experience of the preceding weeks, Witte must have known that these groups would not give in of their own accord. He must have realized that, rather, on the contrary, they were getting ready for a final fight. He must have foreseen this inevitable conflict before he accepted the office of Prime Minister. But he probably hoped for a compromise; he hoped to convince the liberals of the necessity of coöperation even in case they would not be given a free hand to develop the constitutional principles, thus saving— what? Tsardom and the old régime, which was bound certainly to take vengeance on the liberals.

The liberals, on their part, saw very clearly the dangers threatening constitutionalism. From the talks with Witte they realized that he was not able nor even willing to support liberalism because, first, he was trying to defend the monarchy in its most obnoxious form, and, secondly, because he was so very evidently afraid of the Court, of its influences and intrigues, this fear making him utterly unfit to lead any opposition against the reactionaries. And one must acknowledge at present that the worst predictions of the liberals in 1905 came true, justifying their refusal to coöperate with Witte; in his company and under his leadership they could not have saved the situation.

As soon as the liberals definitely refused to enter the new ministry, Witte capitulated to the reactionaries by taking into his cabinet some of their worst representatives, as for example, the Minister of the Interior, P. Durnovo. The government then started to retract its own promises and steadily annihilated the constitutional achievements.

Witte's own atonement, however, came a little later. He was not dismissed at once; the Tsar kept him in office a few months longer for a special reason. It was another proof, this time a glaring one, of how absolutely unreliable Witte was in political matters. This happened at the time of the conclusion of a huge French loan that saved autocracy from imminent bankruptcy. The reactionaries knew that Witte was in good relations with many Western financiers and that some foreign bankers trusted him implicitly. At that moment Russia was in dire need of a loan. Some foreign interest moneys were due, most of the war expenses were still unpaid and internal financial needs became very pressing. Sufficient money could not be realized by taxation, so that the only way out of the trouble was a foreign loan. But the Western bankers were not willing to give money to a dying régime; some of them were openly in favor of a constitutional change in Russia. The ruling groups decided then to make use of Witte in order to allay these doubts, counting on his liberal reputation abroad. It was a very grave mistake of Witte to lend himself to this game and help the reactionaries to protract the death agony of autocracy. He did procure the money in France; but as soon as the government was sure of the loan, he was dismissed, just a few days before the meeting of the Duma.

The first elections gave a strong majority to the liberal center parties, and in particular to the Constitutional Democrats; the two extreme wings, the reactionary right and the socialist left, were relatively insignificant. But even the moderate liberals pressed the government for further concessions. They supported three main claims: first, the establishment of secure guaranties for constitutional freedom and personal liberty, which meant for the government giving up the former police system; secondly, the amnesty of political prisoners, held for all sorts of political offenses; and, thirdly, the granting of land to the peasants.

It was that last claim that alarmed the government more than anything else. In consequence, after a short hesitation a dissolution of the Duma was decided on. A strong man, Stolypin, was appointed Minister of the Interior and intrusted with the practical measures of carrying out the dissolution, which he successfully accomplished. The second elections, as usual in such cases, gave a much more radical majority than previously. Both wings increased at the expense of the liberal center. As soon as the session opened the socialists started violent attacks on the government, claiming much more radical reforms than the Cadets ever had. Having successfully dissolved one Duma, the ministers had no hesitation to repeat the same procedure in the second case. This time, however, in order to avoid getting another radical majority, they changed the electoral law, curtailing suffrage and breaking the constitution. It really meant an open disavowal of the pledges given in October, 1905. Because of the severe police measures taken everywhere, there were, however, very few serious outbreaks of discontentment in the country. The new elections went on quietly and a much more amenable and conservative Duma was the result. The landed nobility, the small gentry and the bureaucracy won the day; it was only the upper classes of the nobility, the aristocracy and the richer landlords who still were among the defeated classes; but they kept on noisily protesting against the wrongs they considered that they were suffering.

Had the government, as Stolypin at first intended, kept to this policy of upholding these middle classes, they might have succeeded in establishing some stable order. They soon succumbed, however, to the pressure of the extreme reactionaries and of the Court; the Tsar himself sympathized with these fanatics and very effectively undermined the authority of Stolypin. The group that supported Stolypin had the sympathies of the conservative Duma and especially of the Octobrist party, representing mostly the afore-mentioned middle classes.

As time went on (1907–1914), the Octobrists gradually became more conservative, whereas the government and the bureaucracy were being rapidly permeated with the worst reactionary elements. Hardly any trace remained of the promised constitutional reforms of 1905; the government was assiduously obliterating them wherever they could be found. Simultaneously, the political persecutions increased in numbers and intensity. But at the same time it was just then that the process of demoralization set in among the police themselves, sapping their power and annihilating the effectiveness of their work. Among the ruling classes degeneration was also rife. On the other hand, the political parties opposed to the government, liberal, radical and socialistic, were becoming steadily better organized, better trained for active work and better equipped theoretically for the defense of constitutionalism.

Neither of the two sides was willing any more to give in. The final struggle thus became inevitable. The ideology of the Revolution was crystallized long ago; the social background for it was now being prepared; the political forces were being mustered and drilled on both sides; and it was only the last outward shock that was still lacking, the spark that would blow up this barrel of powder, quite ready and dry for the explosion. This spark was provided by the events of the Great War, which completely disorganized and demoralized the old régime of the crumbling Empire of the Tsars.

CHAPTER IV

THE EVENTS OF THE REVOLUTION

I

THERE has developed lately a great interest in the psychological phenomena of the crowd, of masses, of the component parts of the social body constituting modern democracies. In former days political science hardly paid any attention to such phenomena, and probably for the simple reason that neither masses nor the people at large played any rôle to speak of in political life. It was usually a small ruling class that decided on policies, constituted the government, and carried out all the functions of administration. Then, in the middle of the nineteenth century, the young science of sociology began to draw the attention of the scientific investigators toward the rôle played by the different other classes, thus widening the circle of research to the different component parts of a nation. The attention of these first sociologists was chiefly directed toward observing outward events, the behavior of the masses, the different class interests, and the way they clashed and interfered with one another. Only later did another group of scientists, the psychologists, realize the one-sided way sociology was treating all of these matters. The psychologists began to see that there was some sort of difference between the way an individual acted when he was alone and when he was placed among other individuals; thus it occurred to them that there existed a really new field for investigation.

Slowly the idea evolved that there could be constructed a special scientific branch of investigation called social psychology, which was in the start a combination of sociology and psychology. Finally, very lately, possibly under the influence of the events of the Great War, new methods of investigation and observation evolved out of the former scientific work.

As a result of that significant advance in these branches of social science, we have at the present day already some very interesting works; for instance: "The Group Mind," William McDougall, 1920; "The Foundations of Social Science," J. M. Williams, 1920; "The Behavior of Crowds," E. D. Martin, 1920.

The Russian Revolution has accumulated in this domain a vast amount of material that still awaits classification and study, and I am convinced that some very important principles will evolve finally for our understanding of the social processes of modern democracy.

There exist three domains of investigation that, to my mind, ought to be studied separately, although naturally they have many points of contact. The first domain is that of ideology and economics, by which I mean the study and classification of ideas and mental processes, on the one hand, and of economic forces that stimulate them, on the other. The second domain would concern the social processes, developing in the social body of a nation. The third domain would have to do with the outward picture of political events, which would comprise the phenomena of the behavior of crowds, government policies, constitutional structure, administration, self-government, and the like.

The first question we meet in this respect is: What is a revolution anyhow? and I think, we have at once to draw an important line of distinction between a revolution and a revolt or uprising. The likeness between them is explained by the similarity of their social meaning; the social processes underlying them are exactly the same ones, the difference being only that the first one supposes a victorious outcome, whereas the latter ends in failure. Both are the direct result of social discontentment and are consequently the expression of a protest against the existing social or political system. Just as with a single individual, if he takes part in a revolutionary movement against his government and fails, he is treated as a criminal, a traitor, or simply a scoundrel, whereas if the movement is victorious (a revolution), the man becomes a hero. The same applies to the crowd, or group, or class that is fighting a government. If the fight is successful and the crowd or group emerges victorious, we have a revolution. If the group is defeated, it is spoken of as a mere mob and soon loses its attraction to the individuals who compose it; they try in consequence, to sever their relations and deny their participation. Nietzsche long ago remarked: "In these cases of failure, former hope for victory becomes an impotent resentment." In Russia we have the best illustrations of such cases and splendid examples of how the crowd-mind worked during the Revolution. In other words, a revolution is a social upheaval that ends successfully in the overthrow of an existing political structure, bringing with it very important and marked changes of a social order too. The *criterion* of a revolution, thus, is the fact of a successful overthrow of a government, which simultaneously is the end of a certain social system. In the vast majority of cases the government pulled down by a revolution was a monarchy, and mostly an autocracy. As was pointed out by E. D. Martin, there exist always two sides to any revolutionary movement that ought to be kept in mind by the investigator. There are, first, the ideas of the revolution that moved the crowds, that are the motive power, sometimes prepared by long decades of political unrest. In most cases we can easily detect the very high idealistic character of these powerful forces. To this factor must be added also the economic forces, acting as a strong incentive to the growth of social discontent. Secondly, we have the outside behavior of the crowds that fight for the above-mentioned ideas and constantly manifest their autocratic tendencies.

Further, we must remember that a revolution never comes unprepared, though the main outbreak can, and often does, come suddenly and at the most unexpected moment. Before the final upheaval, however, there always takes place a long and slow process of growth of the above mentioned social dissatisfaction, a process that develops only very gradually. The most interesting in this respect is the fact that the reactionary climax comes invariably much before the revolution itself, preceding it sometimes by a whole generation or even more. After the climax has worked its worst, there comes a more or less prolonged period of concessions, becoming more and more numerous and important as time goes on. The nearer we get to the moment of the revolutionary outbreak, the weaker we see the attacked government to be, offering sometimes very liberal concessions at the last moment, when it is too late and the discontented nation has no more trust in their decaying government.

The explanation of this is rather simple. The people at large must first experience a reactionary oppression and a selfish dominance of their ruling class or social group. Then they must begin to realize that they are being oppressed. This is the period of the awakening of the people—for instance, the epoch of the great philosophy of France in the eighteenth century. That awakening brings with it the realization of the shortcomings of the existing political system and social order, which starts and fosters the mentioned social dissatisfaction. The latter naturally takes a long time to develop and the larger the nation, the more difficulties would be met by such a process. This is why the ideology of the revolutionary movement takes sometimes such a long period to grow and strengthen.

But this is not sufficient; the ideology of the discontent alone cannot achieve a revolution. The ideology of the Russian movement was quite ripe in the nineteenth century and yet could not bring forth a revolution. Another element is necessary, namely, the active opposition to the autocratic government, the growth not only of the ideas, but of social movements as well, and this, too, takes a long time. These social movements preceding a revolution have usually a double character; on the one hand, they consist in the crystallization of the opposition, in the appearance of opposition parties, organizations, groups, ready to fight the existing political and social systems; and, on the other, the gradual but inevitable decay and degeneration of the social order that is backing the existing government. Growing more selfish, blind in their policy, never heeding the signs of the nation's discontentment, the ruling classes or groups begin steadily to decompose and disintegrate, losing thus their inward strength and being unable to resist the constantly increasing waves of dissatisfaction attacking them from all sides. At the last moment, as was said above, when the danger becomes absolutely imminent, concessions are usually made, liberal reforms grudgingly granted, and promises given, but invariably too late; the nation, and especially its discontented elements, no more believe in such promises and are not ready to accept them as sincere acts, preferring a general clearing out of the whole system.

The Russian Revolution in this respect gives us many interesting examples. The sequence of events in Russia was as follows: The outside history of the Revolution is intimately bound up with the Great War. The revolutionary movement before the war was still very abstract and could achieve relatively little, because the government was still very strong, being able to withstand attacks and hold the movement well in check, and the social discontent was itself not sufficiently active and powerful to accomplish a successful overthrow of the existing system. But with the Great War there necessarily came important changes.

The declaration of war in August, 1914, was accompanied by great enthusiasm. There were no dissenting voices anywhere. The class struggle, all questions of nationalism, all the differences seemed forgotten, and the people everywhere in the country rose spiritedly. It might have seemed for the moment that patriotism was really awakened among the Russian people and that the government, if sufficiently farsighted, would know how to meet the situation. Unfortunately this lasted only a very short time. Then came gradually a feeling of disillusionment, unnoticeable and imponderable at first, but growing in strength and constantly gathering in momentum. In this poisonous atmosphere of suspicions wild rumors began to circulate among the people, and gossip was busy concerning the behavior of different members of the Imperial Family, the ministers, and other high officials. As defeat followed defeat, a feeling of unsteadiness and insecurity began to spread, arousing the fear of the people that the government was not playing a fair game. There is no doubt whatever that the Germans, with their very effective propaganda and spy systems, made the best use they could of these conditions, trying to strengthen the feeling of distrust of the people against their own government.

The German propaganda was working especially strongly on the three following matters: first, the social dissatisfaction of industrial labor; secondly, the political discontent of the bourgeoisie and labor parties; and thirdly, the nationalistic dissatisfaction of the different non-Slavic peoples living in the Russian Empire. Labor was told that the government was intentionally denying them advantages and privileges long ago granted in other Western countries and was imposing upon them the heavy work of war times in order simply to keep them curbed. The educated people, the Russian Intelligentsia, were told that the government was curtailing their civic liberty and even protracting the war in order to fight the ideas and principles of constitutionalism. And, finally, the non-Slavic nationalities were made to feel that their hopes for greater self-government and more independence were futile because the government of the Tsar would always try to impose upon them the feared dangers of centralization. Many individuals, groups, and nationalities unfortunately swallowed the bait of this propaganda with the German hook inside it, and helped very much to strengthen the disintegration of the social structure of Russia, enhancing, thus, one of the preparatory processes of the revolution pointed out above, namely, the inward social decay that necessarily must precede any revolution. On all sides there developed a strong feeling of discontent and fear that was misrepresenting and frightfully exaggerating the social evils existing in Russia, until that dissatisfaction became an overwhelming obsession with the greater part of the people.

And it was just at that moment that there came, in addition to that general unrest, bodily and physical privations that rapidly increased as the months of the war steadily dragged out. Most of the privations in the winter of 1916–1917 resulted from the practical blockade that grew up on account of the policy of the Allied Powers. This blockade cut off the communications of Russia with the outside world; her imports rapidly dropped to very small quantities, with the exception of war materials that were still imported by the Allies in great quantities. Thus, in the autumn of 1916, there rapidly set in a shortage in foodstuffs in all the larger cities of Russia, and especially in the capitals, Petrograd and Moscow. The evils of the growing general shortage were still further increased by the disorganization of transport; the Russian railroads, always weak and inefficient, now began to break down under this new pressure. The government had to use nearly all of the available means of transportation for feeding the army and carrying troops and munitions, and in consequence the distribution of foodstuffs in the Empire began to deteriorate appreciably, increasing immensely the privations of the people.

Meanwhile the government policy, foolish and shortsighted as it was, instead of giving way, heeding the many warnings (and very many indeed they were), and trying to meet the demands of the people, was only increasing the pressure all along the line. No wonder that even the Russian Parliament, the Duma, conservative as it was, began also to show signs of dissatisfaction. The Duma was the only place in the whole empire where a citizen could speak out his mind freely. The labor and progressive minority in the Duma began hence to acquire a wider authority and even started to sway the policies of the Lower House. It was during those months that different labor and progressive representatives delivered very strong attacks against the

Russian government. As time went on, the attacks became more and more violent and outspoken, until the climax came in November, when Deputy Miliukov, in a most drastic way, accused the Prime Minister, Sturmer, and certain Court officials of treasonable acts. The facts that Miliukov mentioned in his speech all tended to show that the stupid reaction of the government played directly into the hands of Germany, that there probably even existed connections or transactions between certain Russians and the Germans, and finally that negotiations with Germany could have been conducted in order to stop the war and save autocracy from unavoidable disaster. The government half-heartedly had to give in, but evidently too late. The revolutionary wave was already spreading fast among the Russians.

II

The revolutionary movement during the Great War, however, did not develop smoothly and evenly. On the contrary, it went by leaps and bounds, the reason being that it was held back by two potent and closely related forces. On the one hand, the so-called *union sacré*, like in all the other countries participating in the war, was welding together the different classes and smoothening out the conflicts of interests in order to strengthen the forces of the nation utilized in and for the war. On the other hand, even among many progressive liberals in Russia, there formed the conviction that a revolutionary outbreak, that would have taken place while the war was still going on fiercely, would have meant a terrible economic disaster for the Russian people. Russia was so weak economically and socially that they thought that she would not be able to stand the strain of both revolution and war at one time and was bound to go to pieces. The worst predictions of our pessimists came true in a worse form than any of them ever expected.

In this unhealthy atmosphere rumors of all sorts, plots and intrigues were rife. There were, in 1916, unguarded accusations directed against the Court and palace surroundings, and chiefly against the Empress. There was nearly open gossip about her German sympathies and German relations. A disastrous rôle was played by the infamous old Rasputin, who had a very great influence upon the Tsarina and who did not make any secret of his pro-German sympathies. His argument was very simple. As he was devoted to the Imperial Family and to the régime that was then in power in Russia, he thought that the only way to curb the constantly growing revolutionary movement was to conclude at once a peace with Germany, so that the government would have the possibility of concentrating all its attention and all its efforts on the curbing of the revolutionary movement. So many people felt and understood the painful significance of the Court intrigues and the obstinate government policy that even among the Imperial Family there were those who tried to convince the Tsar that he should change his policy and get rid of Rasputin. There were two or three attempts made by members of the Imperial Family to talk to Nicholas and open his eyes to the dangers of the situation. The Tsar, however, developed a strange apathy and indifference. He answered such warnings by exiling one of the Grand Dukes from the capital, but took no measures whatever to restrain the activities of his wife. When these men were checked in their efforts, some of them decided themselves to rid the country of him. This is why he was murdered on a December night of 1916. We have also good grounds to believe that there existed different plots and plans among the military, especially the commanding generals, to effect a *coup* by some violent act, getting rid of the Empress and establishing some sort of control over the actions of the weak Tsar himself.

It was at that fateful moment of intense intrigues that the shortage in fuel, in food, and in various other things became unbearable. Very naturally, riots were bound to come. During the winter of 1916–1917, on account of all these warnings, we became convinced of the imminently impending revolution. It was now only a question of time. For those same reasons the police was more or less prepared for such riots, but the government, instead of making some liberal concessions, relied entirely on the backing of the military forces. And it was in this last respect that they were most mistaken. We can assert that a revolutionary outbreak comes usually at the moment when the army, the main military force of the government, either begins to waver or refuses its help to the police.

The revolutionary movement centered from the very first days around the Duma, the only organized semi-popular body then in existence. It was in the terrific confusion of those first revolutionary days, when nobody had any clear point of view and no party nor organization had any well-prepared or thought-out program, that the first provisional government was taking shape in order to receive the reins of power from the dying autocracy. No wonder that this first government was so unprepared for the task and in so many ways proved weak and vacillating. Yet there was also another source of uncertainty contributing to the weakness of this first government, namely, the lack of social backing.

The old régime was crumbling down fast and very effectively. The former officials disappeared, the Tsar abdicated, the police were in hiding, and the members of the new provisional organization, most of them belonging to the Duma, were simply forced to take the power into their own hands. But the mass of the people did not show any great desire to support them. The explanation of that seemingly strange condition lies in the fact that Russia did not possess a strong and solid middle class, a real bourgeoisie, that would have adopted and represented the political and social aspirations of the liberals and progressives, who formed this first government. It was only later, during the long processes of the Revolution, that gradually and painfully such a new middle class began to form, a class not quite crystallized even at the present day. This probably is the most important sociological difference between the Russian and French revolutions, because at the time of the latter France had already a robust bourgeoisie.

The Provisional Government of March, 1917, could satisfy no one. From all sides it was surrounded by enemies and foes. The men whose hearts were with the old régime and whose interests were bound up with autocracy, from the very first naturally tried to interfere in every possible way with the work of the new government. Nor could the more radical elements, the socialists, the representatives of labor and of the peasants, be satisfied by a moderate, liberal program of reforms; they hoped for socialistic achievements and the realization of their lifelong communistic dreams.

During the first days of the Revolution people all over Russia seemed so very happy and content. I shall always remember the genial smile on the face of every man I met in Petrograd or elsewhere at that time. All were sure that at last their day of happiness had arrived. It was that general feeling of release and freedom that invariably comes during the first days of any revolution. How many Russians were mistakenly proud of the "bloodless" revolution and of the easy way the old régime had disappeared. Personally, I could not share this optimism, if only on account of the accidental fact that the few murders that did take place occurred right in front of the windows of our house; the Russian fleet was anchored in the bay facing our house and it was there, on the Russian ships, that many Russian naval officers were killed. The majority of Russians were firmly convinced that the revolution was bloodless.

Then, gradually disappointments set in, when the conflicts of interests and personal grievances began to clash and spoil that radiant impression of the first days. So many people became impatient of the expected happiness not setting in, so many were disappointed because of the lack of realization of their fondest hopes. There is a story told now by Russians that has the significant title, "From Heaven to Hell"; it does really describe how, step by step, the disappointments and disillusionments took the upper hand and created such an opportune source of activity for the most fanatical and uncompromising individuals and groups in the nation that they were bound, sooner or later, to get control over the mass of the people. In this respect E. D. Martin is absolutely right when he points out the striking parallel between the French and the Russian revolutions and the way in which the moderates, who came into power at the beginning, gradually began to lose ground and give way to the more radical and fanatical elements. From Mirabeau the power went to Danton and Carier, from Danton and Carier to Marat and Robespierre; the same exactly in Russia—from Lvov and Miliukov to Kerensky, and from Kerensky to Lenin and Trotzky.

The liberals and progressives invariably produce in revolutionary times weaker and hesitating leaders for the plain reason that they, being educated and having a good knowledge of the outside world, realize the tremendous difficulties that their newly established government has to deal with; they are at the same time little used to government work and ways; they usually have no experience and hardly any endurance. Very naturally do they and must they hesitate in their policies; and it is that hesitation that invariably proves fatal to them. Hesitation is always dangerous for a government, but in revolutionary times it is fatal, and proved so for the Russian Provisional government of 1917. The more radical and unscrupulous leaders easily take the chance and get the upper hand. The usual way it is done is by proclaiming the Revolution in danger on account of the hesitations of the weaker leaders and the evident necessity to replace them by a stronger hand. This is the moment when the dictatorship of the radicals sets in. The Russian Revolution is a wonderful corroboration of that theory.

The attacks of Trotzky and Lenin on the weak Kerensky strongly appealed to the people; they were clamoring to save the Revolution and "deepen its meaning." The radical leaders promised to carry the Revolution to its natural conclusion and give the revolutionary ideas a good chance to spread among the masses of the people.

In order to achieve such a diffusion of revolutionary ideas, the radical or bolshevik group used in Russia the simple but very successful method of appealing to the masses through plain, short and expressive slogans. They used four of them—*Peace, Food, Land,* and *Liberty;* each one meant so much for the poor Russian people. The Russians for some months previously had been longing for peace, for the cessation of the war that they did not and could not understand, and in which they fought without knowing why. What could Russia, even in the case of a brilliant victory, get out of this war?

They also needed food so very much; the blockade and rapid breakdown of transportation were producing in the larger cities a very dangerous food shortage, causing already all sorts of suffering.

And the peasantry, the bulk of the population of Russia, some eighty-five per cent of the nation, was longing for more land for their agricultural needs.

Finally, all classes of the population—peasants and labor, liberals and even many conservatives—had for generations been awaiting the day when they could achieve their political freedom and get some constitutional guaranties for their personal rights and interests.

In other words, these four cleverly chosen slogans were appealing to the greatest needs of the day of the Russian nation at large.

The Provisional government, meanwhile, hampered by its intrinsic weakness, was wavering and tottering, wavering because of their inherent hesitations, and tottering on account of the lack of social support described above. As time went on they became weaker and weaker, and also more and more disorganized. The socialistic elements were gradually taking the upper hand. The more conservative socialists participated in the government of Kerensky, who replaced Lvov as the head of the government in July, and the more radical socialists were active in the soviets, which were steadily getting more influential and powerful.

It was among this last category of socialists that there soon appeared one group, the Bolshevik socialists, who proved strongest and most successful in their policy. As a matter of fact, they were the only small group that had a distinct policy, that knew for what they were standing and what they wanted, wanting it very strongly. They had no moral scruples; they did not stop at the details of daily life, but went straight forward to their beloved aim—the establishment in Russia of a socialistic state and the trying out of a communist experiment.

On account of the weakness of the Kerensky government, the overthrow in November, 1917, came rather
naturally and did not cause the Bolshevik group any
great effort. Then began the third period, of final
destruction of the *ancien régime,* that swept away all
the remnants of the former political and social structure
of the Empire of the Tsars.

III

The winter months that followed the Bolshevik upheaval (November, 1917, to April, 1918) were a period
of drastic and ruthless destruction; the social structure
of the former empire, as well as its whole political system, were being torn down and totally destroyed. The
new rulers, the Bolshevik group, meant to clear the
field for their experiment, driving out and annihilating
all bourgeois and capitalistic elements, wherever they
found them, together with the old ruling classes, the
aristocracy, the nobility and the Tsar's bureaucracy.
During these months of pitiless destruction we can
easily discern the interplay of injured interests that
Mr. Martin so well describes in his book, of the feeling of inferiority of one group as against another, the
dominant group of the moment. There was gradually
taking place at that time a new social readjustment
of the different classes; the Bolshevik group that was
then coming to the front was composed mainly of dis-
gruntled and disappointed individuals, who had suffered badly in one way or another under the Tsar's
régime.* This circumstance made them particularly

* It would be an enticingly interesting subject to study from the
pathological point of view the mental attitude of these leaders.

bitter against the former order of things and extremely
desirous to wipe out all its remnants and inheritances.
Such a state of mind of the Bolsheviki accounts sufficiently for their attacks on Kerensky and his government, whom they accused of compromising with the
ancien régime and desiring to save at least some of its
elements.   Never did they suspect that they themselves, two or three years later, would be forced to do
exactly the very same thing and compromise with the
old bourgeois ways and means of living.

If we apply the above-described sequence of revolutionary events to the incidents that took place in
November, 1917, we can easily see that at that time
Russia lived through a regular second revolution.
Politically it meant that again a new government system came into being, replacing the Provisional government of Kerensky.   It was a revolution because
Kerensky's cabinet was successfully upset by force and
the whole political system that was then in existence
fell to pieces.   Socially it meant the advent of a new
group, very small but very energetic and absolutely
ruthless.   And, finally, economically it was the beginning of a huge experiment in socialism, the establishment of communism, arousing so many hopes, and
yet so little known as to the possible consequences that
it might bring to the nation.   Here we have probably
the greatest lesson that Russia has learned during those
last four years of intense suffering; we can only hope
that this appalling lesson will also prove of some value
to other nations and peoples outside of Russia.

The desire to force the communistic experiment upon
the Russian people was the strongest incentive that

actuated the Bolshevik group, rising then to power, but not even the cleverest among them could foresee how it would work in practice. Then, too, the path they had to tread was in no way a smooth one. Their destructive efforts naturally aroused a strong opposition from those whom they were trying to subdue; the persecuted bourgeois and middle class, for instance, succeeded in thwarting some of the Bolshevik efforts. In self-defense, as they asserted, the Bolsheviki then started a reign of terror, endeavoring to frighten their opponents, or simply destroying them, killing, imprisoning, persecuting, torturing. This is a very usual consequence of the coming to power of a new social group that has to fight for its existence.

But it also naturally leads to the reëstablishment of an autocracy and in its worst form, of dictatorship. It was called by the Bolsheviki, the Dictatorship of the Proletariat. At first it was sincerely meant to represent the proletariat class; very early, however, it proved to be the dictatorship of a small oligarchy only. At present there is no more mystery about this. The Bolshevik leaders openly confess that they intentionally established an oligarchy, that the masses of the people, even the proletarian class included, are never ready to carry the burden of such an experiment and that only the leading minority, they themselves, are able to accomplish the desired results and fulfill the given promises of bringing about a communistic paradise.

Yet it would be a great mistake to exaggerate the forces of opposition that the Bolsheviki met at the beginning of their work; possibly even, on the contrary, the opposition was never very powerful; the old order crumbled away without much difficulty. The aristocracy and former bureaucracy soon disappeared, disintegrated or went into hiding; as to the middle classes, they hardly existed in old Russia.

On the other hand, one must admit that the second, the November revolution, did find a strong social support among two classes at least, the peasantry and labor. Both were staking all their hopes on the new revolution, and as they were very large numerically, their sympathies counted for much. The workingmen were expecting an improvement of their conditions of life and work and were quite sure that the political control would remain forever in the hands of their own representatives. The peasants, on the other hand, hoped mostly for the acquisition of more land, which they needed so badly and which they anticipated would be taken away from the landlords and nobility. Both groups, taken together, amounted to some ninety per cent of the population, the peasants alone constituting about eighty-five per cent. Such high figures easily explain the tremendous strength of social support that the Bolsheviki did have at the beginning. With such a backing they could easily sweep away the remnants of the old régime.

It proved to be, alas, a powerful but exclusively destructive force. The constructive side was conspicuously absent. When the destruction of the old system was successfully accomplished, the Bolsheviki did not find any constructive help forthcoming. The explanation of this is plain: The ideals of communism, for which Bolshevism was standing, did not and could not appeal to either of the two classes just mentioned;

they were ready to support only the destruction of the existing social and political order. The peasants, for instance, were endeavoring to acquire more land, not for any communistic purposes, but in order to own it, to have the free and absolute disposal of it; and when they soon found out that Bolshevism and communism are synonyms and do not in any way guarantee their new landholdings, they quickly started to turn their backs on the Bolshevik government. The latter in consequence speedily lost its strength. The same happened with labor. The new régime did not bring with it the anticipated millennium; improvement of the conditions of life did not set in. On the contrary, these conditions steadily became worse. This caused a great disillusionment among the workingmen and forced many among them to change their views of Bolshevism, weakening in consequence the position of the government.

IV

Considering the events of the Russian Revolution, it is very interesting to note one more important fact, namely, the lack of coincidence between the actual breaking out of the revolution and the reactionary climax of oppression. The latter much preceded the former; it came more than a generation earlier, having taken place in the reign of Alexander III.

With the advent of Nicholas II to the throne, because of his weakness, there started numerous government concessions, tending towards liberalism, but only increasing the impetus of the revolutionary movement. It was these liberal concessions that forced the dominant classes of Russia to weaken their hold over the country and to lose gradually their own prestige. As is so often the case, they could not adapt themselves to new conditions and started on the usual path of intellectual and moral decay. This process of disintegration sooner or later was bound to undermine the old régime. The revolutionary propaganda, to my mind, is only the ferment that helps to further the social disintegration and prevents the ruling classes from rallying their forces at the critical moment and withstanding the last shock. The revolutionary propaganda in such cases makes use of the mystic enthusiasm of crowds, spreading and strengthening the ideals that are bound to play so important a part in the revolution proper and become the ideological background of it.

Still, the success of the revolutionary uprising, even if it establishes its new governmental forms, is usually not a lasting one; further changes must set in before a lasting order ensues. Here again in the case of Russia we find a very instructive example.

The revolutionary movement, like most social movements, has its peak, and after reaching it gradually begins to slacken and die out. And again, one can study these processes from three angles: political, social, and economic. Politically, the old governmental system disappears once and forever. This is decidedly the case with Russia. There is no chance whatever of any elements of the old political order ever coming back. But usually a state comes out of a revolution much more powerful than it was in the years preceding the revolution. The reasons are: first, that it gets a

new political structure better adapted to the new requirements of the day; secondly—and this is more important—the state comes out of a revolution having
become much more impersonal. The vast majority
of revolutions have happened in monarchical countries,
and were aimed at the destruction of monarchy and
autocracy as embodied in the person of one individual,
the monarch, emperor or tsar. After the revolution
and the fall and disappearance of the monarchy, the
state and government become impersonal, and hence
much stronger. Socially, the end of the revolution
means that the new class or group comes to the front
by a violent change, replaces the former ruling class,
and establishes its claims for the future government.
Economically, however, we can see that, contrary to the
two former elements, there remains very much of the
old régime and the changes come much more gradually
and sometimes take a whole generation of human
effort before the new economic forces acquire their
final hold on the people. This is the reason why the
constructive periods that follow a revolution and the
social and economic processes that result from the upheaval are always so slow in developing. They take
sometimes whole decades before a stable new order
finally ensues and the nation that lived through such
a catastrophe enters once more into normal and happy
conditions of life.

CHAPTER V

GERMANY AND THE RUSSIAN REVOLUTION

I

THERE can hardly be any doubt that Germany played a very important rôle in the Russian Revolution, even if she did not create or originate the destructive Bolshevik movement.

We have at present a quite sufficient amount of historical material to be able to judge impartially the activities of the German government in the Russian question. Only one side of these activities still remains somewhat obscure, and these probably never will be disclosed in their entirety; namely, the machinations of the German General Staff. I don't suppose there are more than half a dozen individuals now living who know all the intricate details of the doings in this respect of Ludendorff's Headquarters, and they certainly never will tell the true story. I doubt also whether any written records ever existed concerning the plan to utilize the Russian Revolution for German purposes. Yet this limitation cannot prevent any longer the whole picture of Germany's attitude toward Russia being revealed in all desirable completeness.

True, the history of Germany's policy in this matter is most important, not only for Russia, the victim, but for the rest of the world, as it gives us, first, a clear insight into the all-human side of the Russian Revolution, which stands above the racial or national elements of this social upheaval, and, secondly, it provides us with the opportunity of getting a glimpse into the very depths of the Machiavellian methods used by the German military caste to support and carry out their hateful policy. Did the breakdown and humiliation of 1918 teach the Germans a lesson in this respect? Did the Russian Revolution and their own troubles of 1919 convince the German people that at least some of these events were a direct outcome of the activities of their military commanders? I think the answer is only partly in the affirmative. A few have learned the lesson thoroughly. Another minority group, to which most of the perpetrators belong, never will realize the enormity of their own doings; but the vast majority of Germans necessarily remain indifferent.

Such an indifference or absence of knowledge usually creates a fertile soil for all sorts of rumors, stories and inventions, spread for propaganda purposes. In this case we find a very persistent rumor attributing Bolshevism entirely and exclusively to German intrigues. Bolshevism, we are told, is simply a German invention. This is just as wrong as the assertion that the Bolshevik movement is a Jewish device aimed to wreak vengeance on the Gentiles. The theory of a German invention of Bolshevism brought Russia very harmful consequences; and even at present it has its pernicious reverberations. The main harm was done by diverting the attention of people, Russians and foreigners as well, from the real causes and sources of Bolshevism and thus successfully thwarting many efforts to cope effectively with the movement.

Russia has learned, in consequence of this false theory, a very costly lesson. The movements to crush Bolshevism from the outside by mere force constantly failed and caused a very heavy loss of life, much suffering and severe disappointments.

If the Bolshevik movement had been simply a German invention, artificially created and concocted, it could have been dealt with successfully from the outside and probably would have been crushed in a short time. Instead, being a genuine social process among the Russian people inside the Russian nation, the outside blows only helped to intensify it and make the social class war more bitter, more destructive and more hateful. Social processes, especially those of the scope of the Bolshevik movement, can hardly ever be created artificially from the outside; they can, however, be helped along, canalized, utilized or guided. And this is just what Germany did with Bolshevism. Not having invented or created the movement in any way, the Germans made good use of it, helped the spreading of Bolshevik teachings, assisted cleverly the Bolshevik propaganda, transported Bolshevik agitators, and probably inspired some of their acts and policies. This is quite a different matter from artificially creating a social movement; but it proved just as dangerous and fatal for poor Russia.

II

In German military circles there prevailed long ago two evil convictions: first, that any means are good for the weakening of one's opponent, and that among such means the spread of revolutionary ideas is a very effective one; and, secondly, that Russia in particular, on account of her antiquated political system, was most vulnerable in just that point. They knew, too, how to strike there.

It is well known at the present time, for instance, how many German hopes were built on the ultimate disintegration of the British Empire. Portions of the German war plans were based on the firm conviction that England would never be able to control her dependencies in case of a European war. The reason for the Germans being so very sure of such an outcome was that they were themselves actively stirring up revolutionary movements and social discontent among the British dependencies. They were in constant and close touch with the leaders of these movements; they were carefully studying the theories and effects of colonial dissatisfaction, and in their usual methodical way they were helping along, providing new arguments, finding more justification, vilifying local officials and spreading rumors and calumnies.

Yet, strange to say, they never hesitated on their own account; it never occurred to them that it might be dangerous for their own colonial possessions and subjugated peoples. Was that simply national conceit or the product of their usual blind reliance on brute force and a conviction that if any revolutionary discontent should develop in any of the German dependencies, they would be able to stamp it out mercilessly by ruthless police oppression? Probably both. The tampering with Russia was a trifle more dangerous for

Germany than the intrigues in British colonies, first, because of the proximity of the Russian people, and, secondly, on account of the many points of contact that existed between the two autocracies, Germany suffering from the same political disease and being herself ill adapted to the requirements of modern times. In the Russian question, the German conceit was quite proverbial and overwhelming; the Germans were absolutely convinced that they possessed ample means to prevent at home the troubles they were so effectively fomenting in Russia. Almost universally, the Germans looked down upon the Russians as uncultured barbarians or fantasts; they were firmly convinced that they themselves would never suffer from the ills that afflicted the Russians.

In both cases cited above, in the lack of appreciation of the inner cohesion of the British Empire and concerning the Russians in general and the Russian revolutionary movement in particular, Germany had to learn a severe lesson. These mistakes lost them the war. There is no doubt whatever that had the German government the least suspicion of the possible military strength of the British Empire, and of its ardent participation in the war, Berlin never would have risked the war at all. On the contrary, the German government would have made every possible effort to prevent it. Secondly, concerning Russia, the German mistake cost them the Empire, the Kaiser, and the rule of the military jingoes, the Ludendorffs and company, who were consciously helping the Russian revolutionaries and finally succumbed themselves to the Revolution. Indeed, *habent sua fata acta humana.*

III

The work of the Germans in this field was usually conducted on two parallel lines: they were endeavoring to establish a certain theoretical basis, a system of teachings; and at the same time trying to organize the practical work, mostly propaganda. In the English question, the German professors and scientists were teaching that the downfall of the British Empire was imminent, that all the political and social forces of modern times were tending towards a disintegration of this Empire, that this must be a "natural" outcome. The autonomous colonies never could be expected to give up their independence, and the Germans thought that they would prefer secession to war, severing their ties with the mother-country. In order to substantiate such a theory, the Germans endeavored to foster by all sorts of means the feelings of independence, fomenting discontent with the British rule, convincing the colonials that the only way out of trouble would be the breaking-up of the Empire. In other dependencies, for example, in India and Egypt, the same propaganda was coupled with racial questions. Thus do we find everywhere the same methods, the same objects, and mostly the same effects. Often did it seem before the war that the Germans were right in their assertions. The British Empire appeared to become weaker and less cohesive. But in appreciating the ultimate results the Germans were badly mistaken. The British Empire rose splendidly to the occasion, the colonials fought in the war not less devotedly than

Englishmen; as a result, the bonds of the Empire became stronger and more effective. From the very first day of the war, the British Empire stood up in arms against Germany and displayed such a tremendous and unexpected military power that the Germans must have had a rude awakening from their dreams of pre-war days.

In the case of Russia it developed differently. The German lesson was learned only after some frightful suffering had been caused to the Russian people. Here again German theory worked hand-in-hand with propaganda practice.

It was not the first time that such methods of revolutionary propaganda were applied to Russia. The Russians had their first experience during the Japanese War of 1904–1905. The Japanese used the same German methods of stirring up social trouble among their opponents. Japan spent huge sums of money in supporting revolutionary activities against the Tsar's government. There existed, for instance, a widespread organization in Finland that was fomenting revolutionary uprisings in the north of Russia and was importing arms and ammunition. The Japanese were eagerly helping the revolutionaries to buy arms, to charter steamers (the *John Grafton* was one of those boats; caught by a storm it foundered among the northern islands of Finland), to transport ammunition and men, get passports for them, and so forth. The Finns, excited by the foolish policy of Russification of Finland, were ardently taking part in the movement and were effectively undermining the authority and strength of the Russian government.* The uprising that took place in the summer of 1906 in the fortress of Sveaborg, situated just outside of Helsingfors, the capital of Finland, was the direct result of this movement, though it came too late for the Japanese, peace having been concluded the previous autumn. The unfortunate incident of the Dogger Bank in the North Sea, when the nervous Russian admiral fired on defenseless English fishing craft, is another instance of the same kind. It was Japanese propaganda that was endeavoring to convince the Russians of the existence of Japanese torpedo boats in the North Sea. This scared the Russians out of their wits and created trouble with England. The Japanese came very near scoring a great success. In case of war between England and Russia the English fleet would have blocked the way for the Russian squadron, sent out to fight the Japanese in the East, and probably would have annihilated it.

It is hard to tell at present if these methods of stirring up revolutionary activities in the camp of the enemy were taken by the Japanese from the Germans or vice versa. One thing is sure, however: in both countries the military commanders considered such methods a valuable and necessary war asset. They used them, not seeing anything bad in them and not realizing that in most cases these methods prove to be a boomerang and sooner or later come back to hit the one who started them. The German military authorities had carefully studied the methods used by the Japanese in 1904–1905, improved upon them, and ruth-

* Comp.: Konni Zilliacus, "The Russian Revolutionary Movement," 1905, and A. M. Pooley, "Japan's Foreign Policy," 1920.

lessly applied them to Russia during the Great War. But the policy did prove to be a boomerang; it hit Germany later on by the spread of the revolutionary poison. The social disease that is created by this poison proved to be an extremely contagious one; in their conceit the Germans felt very sure of being able to prevent its evils, but were badly mistaken. The disease began to spread in 1918 and 1919 with appalling rapidity among the German people themselves. Only after heroic measures had been taken in 1919 did they succeed in stopping it.

IV

The German government started to use the methods of stirring up a revolution in Russia during the early months of the war, in the autumn of 1914. We have no evidence of their systematic application before that, though preparatory measures were certainly being taken. Yet there always existed in times of peace a great deterrent for Germany to use such methods on account of Germany's own autocratic system. Not only did the revolutionary movement weaken the Russian government *per se*, but it was evidently able to shake the confidence of nations in autocracy all over the world. Before the war this had some serious repercussions even in Germany, where the socialistic movement was constantly growing in strength and protests against the rule of the Kaiser were becoming much more frequent. Then, too, there existed the family bonds: the Tsar was closely related to the German ruling houses. At times, the Romanoffs were very friendly to the Hohenzollerns; many of them inter-married and lived together in harmony. For these reasons it must have seemed dangerous for at least some Germans to undermine the prestige of the Tsar and his government. In consequence, the Berlin government did not press the matter and was content to take only preparatory measures. In this last respect, the support of nationalistic movements among the non-Slavic elements of the Empire of the Tsars was probably Germany's most important object previous to 1914.

But all this suddenly changed, the moment war was decided upon. From that day on there existed no more scruples for Berlin concerning the Romanoff family, no more hesitation for the German government relative to the weakening of the monarchical principle in Russia. As to moral considerations, they never existed anyway for the German government.

The Russian armies did not seem very formidable to the German generals; they thought that the Russians could be easily checked. In consequence, the military problem resolved itself in the gradual weakening of the nation itself; in undermining its powers of resistance and shaking its morale, tiring it out by constant but futile efforts. The resistance of the Russian army proved, however, far more efficient and powerful than the Germans had ever expected; and this tended to prolong the process of dissolution that the Germans were fostering. This unexpected resistance that the Germans met on the Russian front was also one of the most potent causes for the lengthening of the war in general and saved the Allies in the west.

The Germans had, in consequence, to redouble their

efforts to demoralize the Russian nation. They conducted this work on three parallel lines; first, by assisting through all sorts of means the numerous Russian revolutionaries outside of Russia; secondly, by
fomenting dissatisfaction inside of Russia; and, thirdly,
by endeavoring to increase the discontent of the non-
Slavic peoples of the Empire.

The war caught quite unaware very many Russian
revolutionaries living in exile. On account of the police
persecutions in Russia there were vast numbers of
such exiles living in many of the larger cities of Western Europe. Most of them very soon after the beginning of the war migrated into Switzerland, where
most of their parties had established their headquarters. Only very few of these men, the better educated
ones, and those who were less fanatic in their party
allegiance and knew better the trend of development
of the modern West-European countries, realized the
situation in its full scope and saw the dangers that
might threaten Europe in case German autocracy won
the war. They also realized the danger that was threatening Russia in case Germany should gain the upper
hand. There would never have been any chance in
such an eventuality for Russian constitutionalism to
develop. Russia would have been subdued, vanquished
and cowed under some worse form of Tsarism, autocratic and centralized. The men of this very small
group, like Plehanoff, Kropotkin, and a few others, took
in consequence and unreservedly the side of the Allies;
they accepted the idea of a "sacred union" of all political parties as it was preached in France and England.

The other Russian revolutionaries and socialists did

not see it at all in this light. They were inclined to hope for a defeat of Russia as being the only means of getting their freedom. Their favorite argument was that liberalism and reforms came in Russia only as a consequence of military humiliation; such was the case of the Crimean defeat of 1855 and the Japanese victory of 1905. They considered that only a national catastrophe could help to extort from the Russian autocracy the hoped-for radical reforms. It was this disastrous idea that the German propaganda was endeavoring to strengthen and support. Some of the Russian exiles were consciously made use of by the German agents, others were blinded by their hatred of the Russian government, their fanaticism not allowing them to realize their mistakes. On the whole, one can say that the Germans had an easy job. They soon succeeded in starting a strong "defeatist" movement among the Russian exiles in Switzerland, spreading the same ideas also in some Allied quarters.

It was in accordance with this activity that special "defeatist" meetings took place in Switzerland, in Zimmerwaldt (1915), and in Kienthal (1916), where the Russian question was violently debated and well-known resolutions passed, calling for the defeat of Russia as the only possible means of achieving any liberty and progress in the east of Europe. Switzerland was full of German agents at the time, and many of them took the most active part in the affair. It was there that the Russian Bolshevik group started its activity and Lenin undertook its new leadership. At that moment the Germans were playing a sure game; they had no fear whatever of those ideas reaching their own country.

The frontier was hermetically closed, the censorship in Germany was in absolute control of the press and of the news-service. Probably most Germans never even heard of those meetings. The German police was so overwhelmingly strong that only few could discuss defeatism in Germany. In Russia, on the contrary, it had a disastrous effect. Thanks to the German propaganda going on in Russia, the ideas of Zimmerwaldt soon became known to the Russian radicals and socialists at home and won many followers. The shortsighted oppression of the Tsar's government helped to strengthen the growing dissatisfaction; it was a brilliant argument for the extremists, contending that the Russian ministers and the Tsar himself would never reform of their own free will, and that only a military defeat would force them to change; consequently, they increased their efforts in this respect.

Up to 1916 the work of the German agents in Russia was very carefully concealed and conducted on a restricted scale only. The Germans could not have many agents in Russia; the Russian military control was still efficient and succeeded in combing out many German spies and organizations; but as time went on and the Russian government became weak and tottering, the German propaganda became much more effective.

For the purpose of facilitating it and keeping connections in Russia, Germany utilized a back-door entrance into Russia by way of Scandinavia and Finland. It was a part of an old German plan existing probably many years previous to the Great War of 1914. Germany had a well-organized system of agents in Sweden who made it their business to keep this back door permanently opened.   They endeavored to create ill feeling between the Swedes and Russians by cleverly spreading all sorts of news about Russia's aggressive plans, concerning her desire to wrest from Sweden or Norway a northern harbor, conquer more Scandinavian territory, and so forth.   There was much talk for some years about an apocryphal testament of Peter the Great; it was believed that this Tsar had contemplated the acquisition of a part of the Arctic coast and instructed his heirs to conduct the same policy.   One must admit that the German propaganda was in many ways successful; it did arouse the Swedes, unfortunately not without the foolish help of the Russian government itself.   Worst of all in this respect was the criminal Russian policy in Finland.   Instead of establishing friendly relations, the Russians alienated the Finns by their coercion and stirred up so much hatred among the Finns, that the latter became easy victims to the German propaganda.   It was just the thing that Germany wanted and expected.   The moment Finland became inimical to Russia a very useful channel of communications into Russia could be established via Finland.

Ludendorff in his "Memoirs" mentions these facts but asserts that he really did not expect the Russian Revolution to take place; he even tries to deny any responsibility in fomenting it.   This, however, can be easily disproved, particularly by the confessions of another general, his subordinate, Hoffmann, who was in charge of the Russian section of the German General Staff.   What Ludendorff really did not expect was the spread of revolutionary ideas in Germany; as to Russia, he never had any hesitations whatever.

Parallel to this propaganda the Germans used the third method mentioned above, that of supporting the nationalistic unrest wherever they could. It was an old idea of the Germans, originating in the time of Bismarck. As a consequence of many conquests Russia had absorbed many different non-Slavic nationalities. Bismarck's plan was to make use of these nationalities in order to weaken Russia. The Russian government, as though on purpose, met this plan by constantly alienating the border-peoples and creating among them national hatred against Russia. This could have been so easily avoided or prevented by making timely concessions to the nationalities, by granting them local self-government and national autonomy; but this the Russian autocracy never realized and never would do. Such a farsighted policy was too much against the grain of autocratic pride and bureaucratic principles.

v

Thus the German policy was most successful in two instances, in Finland and in Galicia. In the first case, the Germans acted through Sweden and kept up elaborate "Intelligence" organizations in the north in order to penetrate into Russia in times of war. In the second case, Austria was used for a similar purpose. Long before the war, the Vienna government had helped to organize on the Polish frontier, near Cracow, Russian socialistic and radical centers. Among the participants of the latter we find the names of many present-day Bolshevik leaders: Lenin, Zinoviev, Kamenev and others were quietly living there, conducting their harmful propaganda. In addition, there was organized in Vienna another movement, the so-called Ukrainophiles, who stood for an independent Ukraina under the possible guidance of Austria. In other words, we have in Galicia exactly the same picture as in the north. Through the socialistic organizations in the vicinity of Cracow, Vienna and Berlin were constantly kept informed as to the growth and spread of social discontent in Russia, and by means of the Ukrainophiles they were endeavoring to stir up nationalistic dissatisfaction among the Little Russians of the south; and again the Tsar's government foolishly lent itself to the accomplishment of these plans by a reactionary policy of suppression of the Ukraina movement. The people of the Ukraina would have been easily satisfied by a grant of local autonomy.

As soon as war broke out in August, 1914, these two channels of communication with Russia became invaluable for the Teutonic Powers. They had thus successfully organized a useful opening into the interior of Russia and were able to foment no little trouble in that distracted country.

The German High Command realized at once the splendid chance that came to them in March, 1917, after the Tsar had abdicated. The German generals in consequence decided to make the best use of it that they could. They set to work all their agents and organizations that were living among the Russian exiles, in Switzerland and in other places, instructing them to make every possible effort to induce and convince the

Russians of the advisability of going immediately home to Russia. Ludendorff's Headquarters in doing this were absolutely sure that the return of all these fanatical radicals would create a lot of trouble in Russia, from which Germany was bound to profit. As has been said, they had no fears for their own country, which they deemed sufficiently immune and well under their control; whereas in Russia, they knew that the arrival of such masses of extremists would spread the social poison of dissatisfaction all over the country and necessarily lead to the ultimate collapse of the Russian army. But in order to be on the safe side, the Germans transported these Russians across Germany with special precautions so as to avoid any possible contact with the local population. They kept them on board a special train, well guarded by detectives and officers; no outsider was allowed to approach without a special permit, and no communications were permitted between these Russian travelers and the German people. Thus there originated the legend of a "sealed train" crossing Germany with the Bolshevik bacillus in it, ready to be planted in Russia for the rapid spread of the Bolshevik disease. The cars naturally were never sealed at all, but the Bolshevik passengers before leaving Switzerland took a written pledge not to have any communications with the outside world while traveling across Germany.* The German Staff acted in this case very much like a doctor or chemist handling dangerous poisons or bacteria; the Germans did it method-

---

* Karl Radek, one of the Bolshevik leaders and participant in this remarkable trip, gives us in his usual cynical way the details of the voyage. See *Die Rote Fahne*, January 3–4, 1922, and the *Living Age*, February 25, 1922.

ically and in perfectly cold blood, inoculating Russia with the most terrible social disease.

This is the one thing that the Russians probably will never forgive the German military commanders. No excuses of Ludendorff and Hoffmann, the two chief culprits, will ever exonerate them from having used such foul methods; they knew quite well what they were doing.

On the other hand, the psychology of the Russian Bolsheviki, Lenin and his fellow travelers, can be explained very easily. During these past years there has been much talk about their treachery; some people asserted that these men were simply German agents paid with German money; it was said that they took the German money and agreed to German help from mere cupidity. Their real motives were, however, quite different ones. They never were simple agents of Germany, though the Germans evidently made very good use of them. Lenin never denied either that he received the money from the Germans* and that he willingly accepted their offer of transportation; in fact, he acknowledged this at the very beginning of the Revolution. But—and this is the main point—he and his friends were perfectly convinced that they were fooling the Germans and that the day was very near when they would be able to repay this ugly debt by starting a revolution in Germany too. Radek, in his recent confession, states this very clearly. "Of

* General Hoffmann tells in his "Memoirs" of having handed over several million rubles to these men while they were on their way to Russia. One has no reason to doubt this statement, which is corroborated by many other facts, though the exact amount of money given to Lenin still remains unknown.

course," he says, "we knew perfectly well that the German authorities had their own designs in granting us the permission to travel across Germany [Indeed they did!] . . . . We did not pay much attention to this, for we knew that if a true proletarian revolution developed in Russia, its influence would spread far beyond our borders." We have here, in a nutshell, the psychological crux of the whole situation. Lenin asserted repeatedly that he would take money or help from any one as long as it could serve his purpose of overturning the capitalistic régime wherever possible. He denies, somewhat as the Germans did when they justified their actions in this war, that moral principles should play any rôle in politics. According to him, no moral valuation of any political acts can ever be admissible.

Further, there cannot be any doubt that there came with Lenin some genuine German agents who were regularly in the employ of the German General Staff, and possibly he knew about it; but it did not affect this fanatical leader, because he was so absolutely sure of his final victory in Russia as well as in Germany. And at present one must acknowledge that he came very near to a brilliant success.

The plan of taking vengeance on Germany was a rather simple one. As soon as a communistic millennium was started in Russia, Lenin argued, no other nation would be able to resist the temptation of following this example. This was, according to him, especially the case with Germany, because of her own autocratic régime that fostered great discontent among the Germans; Lenin was convinced that they would rise against their government at the first opportunity.

Later events in Germany prove that he was not very far wrong! The Bolshevik poison always was extremely contagious; no land frontiers, customs cordons, or police obstructions can stop the spread of revolutionary ideas. Lenin was certainly much nearer to reality than Ludendorff and Hoffmann ever had been. His only miscalculation was the belief that the German revolution was quite inevitable and that the German people would rise in case of victory as well as in consequence of a defeat. Lenin never understood, in other words, that a German victory, the main hope of the Teuton generals, would have strengthened tremendously the Berlin autocracy, and that in that case no revolution in Germany would have been possible. On the whole, it was a terrible gamble, the fates of whole nations being at stake.

VI

The Russian Bolshevik refugees, having reached their country, had to be supported further in their destructive work. The German High Command had thus to furnish the necessary means, using the above-mentioned channels of communication through the north. On account of the revolutionary troubles and the ensuing disorganization of the Russian government machine, such connections in 1917 were made relatively easy for the Germans. The government of Kerensky was absolutely powerless to fight these activities. The Germans then concentrated their efforts on one object, the destruction of the Russian army.

In Finland at the same time they were endeavoring to demoralize the Russian battle fleet. The German agents easily permeated the personnel of the navy, successfully undermining the authority of the command and officers. Many of the latter—and the very best among them—were murdered.

There was a moment, in July, 1917, when Kerensky seemed to have a chance of making a clean sweep of these organizations. The Ministry of Justice disclosed a whole nest of them and discovered the channels through which the money was being sent from Sweden to Russia, through the German bureau in Stockholm and agents in Finland. Documents of vast importance were found, names of some agents were made public; but nothing was accomplished in the matter of criminal prosecution. The Bolshevik leaders for a short time went into hiding. Lenin and Trotzky suddenly disappeared from Petrograd, where they had previously been living quite openly, but no measures were taken either to find or to prosecute them, and in a very short while they returned to the capital and renewed their infamous work. It was at that time that Kerensky proved so very weak; he could not cope with the situation at all.

After the downfall of Kerensky, the Germans came into Russia without any hesitation or disguise. One could see them in the streets of Petrograd, sometimes wearing the German uniform. They did not care much about what was going on in government matters; the Bolsheviki had a free hand to destroy the old régime and establish their rule, starting their communistic experiment. But the Germans did care very much about the Russian army; they were intent on finally destroying it in order to take away all their own troops from their eastern front and concentrate them against the western Allies.

This work was accomplished during the winter months of 1917–1918. The Russian army was melting away very rapidly and of course could not make any effort to resist the pressure of the Germans. The Bolsheviki looked on complacently; they could not help themselves; they were completely overwhelmed by the Germans. But the destruction of the old army must have pleased them, as it removed any possible danger of a military attack on their government.

Meanwhile, peace transactions were started by the Germans. The Bolshevik leaders very soon realized that Germany now was extorting a high price for the help given to these fanatics during the preceding months. Germany now wanted the full control of Russia and treated the Russians like a vanquished foe. Trotzky tried all sorts of devices, sometimes joking, sometimes bullying, but to no avail; he had to yield finally and sign the disgraceful and humiliating peace conditions of Brest-Litovsk.

This was the last staggering blow given by Germany. She had, consequently, the complete mastery of the situation, though only for a short time; only as long as she herself was still sure of her final victory. The German ambassador in Moscow, Count Mirbach, could do what he pleased and shamelessly conducted his intimidating policy. But as soon as Germany began to weaken on the western front she was forced *eo ipso* to let go of her control over Russia. Toward the autumn of 1918 it became evident that Germany would be beaten and cowed in the west; as a result, her control of the Russian government quickly evaporated and disappeared.

It is interesting to note that in specifying her conditions at Brest-Litovsk, Germany realized the main points of Bismarck's old plan concerning the border-states of Russia. These border-states received their independence from Russia but remained under the control of Germany. Germany certainly did not do this for their sake, having in view only her own advantages. The whole situation was an extremely profitable one for Germany; as long as the border-states were under German control the Germans could use them for two purposes: they could exert a strategic pressure on Russia; having control of the Baltic Sea they could easily transport any amount of troops into these border-states, concentrate them along the coast and attack Russia at any point. Secondly, the border-states were an excellent doorway into Russia for economic purposes; the Germans could penetrate hence into the interior of the Russian markets, get there the Russian raw materials, and in exchange dump on these markets the products of their own industries.

After the murder of Count Mirbach, the German ambassador to Moscow, the German government was no longer sure of its policy toward Russia. There were at the time two parties in Germany with very different political programs concerning the Russian situation.* One party was proclaiming that Germany

* Comp. for instance, the "Memoirs" of Helfferich, the successor of Mirbach in Moscow and former Vice-Chancellor of the German Empire.

ought to endeavor in the future to unite the anti-Bolshevik forces of Russia and assist the efforts to overthrow the Bolshevik government; they argued that Bolshevism had done its work, that it had become only harmful for Russia and dangerous to the outside world, Germany included. They were no longer sure of themselves at home. To their amazement, revolutionary propaganda was beginning to spread in Germany also. On the other hand, they thought that coöperation with a non-Bolshevik Russia would be of great advantage for Germany in the future. Germany could retain some sort of control over Russian affairs and successfully exploit the national resources of Russia, finding there a friendly ally against the Western Powers. These men had especially in view the possible competition with England for the control of Russian markets. The second group, on the contrary, stood for a close coöperation with the Bolshevik government. These men were very much afraid of the future regeneration of Russia; they considered that a weak and dismembered Russia was of great advantage to Germany and that Berlin would find it much easier to control a weak Russia. Their hopes were built entirely on the subservience of the Bolsheviki, though the murder of Mirbach might have been a fair warning in this respect.

The first of the two parties wielded the stronger arguments, and its political victory would have proved a great danger for the Western world. The Germans would have acquired in such a case a tremendous power over Russia, which could have lasted a very long time and certainly would have been a source of great strength for Germany. It was the second group, however, that won the day in 1918 and imposed its policy on the German government. Their main argument, the one that seemed to have convinced the Berlin government, was that a resurrected Russia would invariably tend toward the west and shun the friendship of Germany and that, therefore, keeping Russia weak was the best policy for Germany.

Thus, up to the armistice Berlin was endeavoring to support the Bolsheviki. The latter were allowed to send an Embassy to Berlin and soon gave the Germans a new proof of how dangerous their teachings were and how contagious the Bolshevik disease really was.

The Bolshevik Embassy, with Joffe at its head, started an intense propaganda in Germany and soon was successful in fomenting there social discontentment. The German government for a time, being so sure of itself, did not believe that such a propaganda was possible, though the police had some inklings of it and gave due warning, until finally a Bolshevik courier was arrested at a railway station, having in his possession a satchel full of the most venomous propaganda literature. Severe measures were hurriedly taken, but evidently too late; the Bolshevik microbe was already planted in the body of the German people.

Just at that time came the final breakdown of the German military force, and at once the poison of Bolshevism began its destructive work. Revolution followed, upsetting the German Imperial government and proving a momentary success for Lenin's theories and hopes. For two or three months, early in 1919, it seemed that he did avenge himself of Ludendorff.*

The above-mentioned facts prove sufficiently clearly what a dangerous and immoral game the German generals were playing when they helped to spread the revolutionary ideas in Russia. It is always an extremely dangerous gamble, but in the case of Germany it was bound to prove disastrous on account of the shortcomings of her own political system. Germany herself had an objectionable autocracy ruling the nation, which gave Lenin his chance to gamble. Meanwhile poor Russia was the loser on both sides on account of her political and economic weakness.

Thus we see that in the end the Russian Revolution, though not created or originated by Germany, was very effectively supported by the German military caste to its own detriment and to the ruin of Russia. In the end the Germans did not profit from it either; their game was based on the firm conviction of a final victory. But as soon as the war was lost, Germany simultaneously lost her game in the East. Seldom in history have foul political means brought with them such striking retribution and atonement.

*Comp. G. Noske, "Von Kiel bis Kapp." The author, who was the leading figure on the moderate side during the German Revolution, gives a graphic account of the working of the Bolshevik bacillus in Germany.

CHAPTER VI

SOME LESSONS OF THE RUSSIAN REVOLUTION

THE more one studies history, the more one becomes convinced of how little nations learn from the experience of other peoples, states or societies. As the cycles of culture follow one another, the same old story of unlearned lessons repeats itself almost with mathematical precision. In former days, however, there was one good excuse; the science of history hardly existed, and certainly did not elucidate the social and political processes of the past. At present, in this respect we can witness an important advance; people can be, if they want, much better informed as to the past of other nations. The science of history has developed very effective methods of investigation, it has explored many unknown regions and furnished information concerning many historical events and social processes. And yet, as stated above, most lessons of history are entirely lost to the world and others are purposely distorted or misused. The great historical events, such as revolutions or wars, are the most glaring instance of these cases. In revolutions, for example, there are many most important elements that have a decidedly all-human character, standing above nationality or race, and that alone explains the numerous similarities that

130

exist between a French, Russian or American revolution. And it is just these all-human characteristics that could serve as lessons to other nations and could teach them how to do some things and to avoid others. No longer can there be any doubt at present that not only political events but also social processes can be influenced and rationalized by conscious efforts of will of the awakened individual.

Another most important point to be kept in mind is the fact that culture and civilization develop by cycles, whatever we think of human progress in general. These cycles come and go, being separated from one another by periods of distinct relapse and breakdown, when sometimes barbarism looms up at the door of most highly civilized nations. The most remarkable instance of this is the downfall of Rome. After the Roman Empire had conquered the Barbarians, barbarism began to percolate into the body of the Roman nation and gradually permeated it, bringing with it a decline of general culture, loose morals, selfishness of the ruling classes and degeneration of state and society. During these days of decay the barbarians were even asked to help and played the rôle of advisers and friends, until the whole Roman civilization seemed to have crumbled away forever. Only after long and "dark" centuries of struggle do we find the first signs of Renaissance and of a new civilization growing up again.

The Russian Revolution has brought with it some improvements of the social order that have come to stay and may be looked on as important and useful acquisitions. To deny this would be shortsighted and unfair. But with the improvements came also destructive forces, perhaps of only temporary duration and of no great outside influence, but still pernicious and evil in their effect. That, I think, is the first important lesson to be learned from what is happening in Russia at this moment. The destructive forces must be fought without hesitation and fear for the social and political improvements achieved by the Revolution. If the latter have any intrinsic value they will survive and be victorious in the end; counteracting the evil forces may only help the development of such improvements.

Among the evil forces of the Russian Revolution, Bolshevism is certainly the most dangerous one, a pathological excrescence on the body of the Revolution; intimately bound up with it and yet not belonging in any way to its essence, it brought with it only destruction and suffering. In the French Revolution we have a similar case. The French Terror was also a pathological addition to the healthy social processes, thwarting and hampering the course of the latter. The French Terror brought with it immense suffering to whole classes of the population, but now that many decades separate us from these events we can judge better, in the historical perspective, its meaning to the French nation in general. No serious historian will ever confound the Terror with the Revolution.

There may be only one doubt left, namely, as to how unavoidable these bloody events are in any revolution. Are they a necessary component part or not? If the main achievements of a revolution, in destroying an obnoxious and antiquated old régime and helping to create a new social and political order, are an improvement and a step forward in a nation's life, must they come, as all improvements usually do come, only at the price of suffering? The history of most revolutions seems to justify an affirmative answer, though it might seem and feel a wicked assertion, especially for contemporaries who had to live through such painful events.

It took a long while—some four years—for the outside world to learn that lesson, of the absolutely necessary distinction to be made between the baneful and dangerous developments of these last years and the distinct improvements in the social and political life of the Russian nation brought by the Revolution. Unfortunately, public opinion was repeatedly swayed by contradictory rumors.

On the one hand, all those who stood for the old régime or were afraid for some reason or other of the new ideas and institutions, were very much alarmed by the destruction wrought by the Revolution and were firmly convinced that the pernicious forces of Bolshevism permeated the whole revolutionary processes. Consequently, these people attacked and vilified both Bolshevism and Revolution, endeavoring systematically to confound them. On the other hand, many progressive and radical elements, especially abroad, made the opposite mistake, also identifying Bolshevism with the Revolution, but the other way, blindly asserting that both of them were inherently beneficial and likewise praiseworthy. They tried to prove that all information tending to disclose the destructive results of the Bolshevik rule were purely reactionary propaganda, meant to abuse the Revolution in general, and strove, on their side, to glorify Bolshevism in theory and assist it in practice. There were good reasons, too, for such an assumption. The reactionaries did mix up matters, as has just been said. Liberal and progressive Russia suffered extremely from such a misunderstanding of its purposes by so many foreigners. The Bolshevik government, on the contrary, made good capital out of this mistaken support. For a long time it was the source of valuable moral encouragement to the Bolsheviki; sometimes it really meant even practical help.

Only very gradually during these recent months has the lesson been learned in other countries, at the cost of great suffering in Russia. The outside world slowly began to realize the scope of the havoc brought about by the Bolshevik rule, and that Bolshevism was in no way the "essence" of the Russian Revolution. Then, too, there unfortunately existed people, inside and outside of Russia, who took advantage of the above-mentioned blunders, identifying Bolshevism with the Revolution for their own selfish purposes.

All this explains many serious mistakes of Russia's former Allies and the harm their policies have done to Russia. It elucidates, for instance, the constant waverings and hesitations, swinging from uncompromising hatred of Bolshevism and Revolution to attempts at dealing with the Bolshevik government as a possible partner in the Comity of nations. In such cases the Allies did not draw the necessary line of distinction between Bolshevism and Revolution, repeatedly identifying them and siding either with the reactionaries and conservatives in frantically condemning both, or else supporting the cause of Bolshevism by confounding it with the Revolution, according to the views of Bolshevik admirers. It explains, further, how certain governments expected to alleviate the evils of unemployment in their own countries and also counted on getting raw materials out of Russia, while Russia herself needed them so very badly. It explains, too, why certain prime ministers were still hoping to get food supplies out of Russia when Bolshevism, as an economic system, was causing famine and starvation.

The Bolshevik government naturally was extremely keen to help these processes. Support of Bolshevism was explained by the fear of anarchy that would necessarily come, so it was said, with the downfall of the Bolsheviki; but, as a Russian writer said some time ago, isn't the bogy of anarchy the usual argument in defense of all autocracies? Isn't it invariably used by pharisees and autocrats, who deny revolution and prevent opposition to any tyranny? Indeed, *malo periculosam libertatem quam quietam servitutem!*

Finally, where is the proof that the downfall of Bolshevism necessarily will lead to anarchy? Only and exclusively in the claim of a few foreigners who have lately come out of Russia and have not seen any signs of opposition to the Bolshevik rule. But could they have seen it, even if it did exist? And where is the proof that it cannot start to-morrow? It reminds one involuntarily of the arguments of foreigners some ten or fifteen years ago, concerning the strength of the Tsar's autocracy; not one foreigner in a thousand foresaw the coming change. On the surface the Tsar's government was one of the strongest in Europe, having a stable social order back of it, a splendid army, a very efficient police and spy system, and last but not least, a firm historical background, three hundred years of existence. No wonder the best informed foreigners doubted the coming revolution. The whole policy of some of Russia's former Allies was built on just that assurance, notwithstanding the many warnings to the contrary.

In other words, the most baneful consequence of this confusion was the weakening of the Russian liberal and progressive stand that alone could lead to a democratic regeneration of Russia.

Another important lesson that Russia and the world can learn is the fact that a revolution comes only when the army begins to waver and lose its military discipline. It is the spark that brings forth the revolutionary outburst. There must be a long, protracted and painful process of social dissatisfaction, political instability, economic defects and evils, preparing the revolution; but the class or social group that is for the time being the foundation and support of the existing political order and government can eventually continue to rule over the other classes of the population, even if it is itself degenerating and losing its social strength, as long as it still can control the army. Even the police system might deteriorate and become inefficient, yet the ultimate fate of the existing political order would depend exclusively on the army. All autocratic governments know that and are careful to keep the army satisfied, in good condition, and, in particular, under severe military discipline. As soon as the latter begins to give way, one can be absolutely sure that the social dissatisfaction of a country has entered into its last stage of development and that a revolutionary outburst is not far distant. Sometimes the decay of military discipline comes very gradually and slowly, approaching step by step the final breakdown, but once such decay has set in, it is incurable and the end is bound to come sooner or later.

The Russian Revolution corroborates brilliantly this statement. The development of the revolutionary movement, on the one hand, and the gradual degeneration of autocracy, on the other, were slowly proceeding for many years, and still no end was in sight as long as the government could control the army. The Russian political police was failing very fast, especially after the first revolutionary outbreak of 1905; corruption, methods of provocation, selfish interests and internal intrigues became dominant in the police system during the period of 1906–1914. Stolypin, the Prime Minister and chief of the secret service, himself fell at the hand of a minor police agent who was playing the double game for and against the revolutionaries. The famous case of Asef, the well-known *agent-provocateur*, is another instance of this degeneration of the Russian police. And yet, autocracy could maintain itself as long as the Tsar and his ministers could rely on the army and use it for coercive purposes.

But when the Great War broke out, two consequences soon became evident. First, the army was wholly occupied by the war; in many provinces there were no more regiments available to quell disturbances and the police were left to their own devices, which soon proved insufficient. Secondly, the army itself, as the long months of war dragged on indefinitely, began to show signs of discontent. The government, realizing the seriousness of the situation, tried to allay the dissatisfaction by attending to the bodily needs of the soldiers. In no war of Russia were her soldiers so well cared for as during the first two years of the war with Germany; they were well fed, clothed and housed, and, on the whole, lived better than these peasant boys ever did at home, in their villages. It was only ammunition that was disastrously short; this was bound to influence the morale of the army. In the Western countries there also came a moment when the Allies were dangerously short of ammunition, but their splendid patriotic effort and the united exertions of the nations, who rose so beautifully to the occasion, saved the situation. In Russia, on the contrary, the endeavors to unite the nation constantly failed on account of the rising tide of social dissatisfaction. In the army there was no understanding of the aims of the war; the soldiers did not know for what they really were fighting and sacrificing their lives. As defeat followed defeat and no end of the war was ever in sight, the morale of the army began to waver and the military discipline became slack.

Meanwhile, the government was foolishly calling to the colors more and more men, urged in this short-sighted policy by the impatient Allies, who staked so many hopes on the mere numbers of the Russian army, until the moment came when the Tsar's government, itself decaying and tottering, could no more control the millions of recruits it had assembled in the larger cities.

That last circumstance helped the spread of discontent very much; in the big towns the revolutionary propaganda could reach the masses of recruits much more easily than in the villages and country places. All through the winter of 1916–1917 the discontent with the government was rapidly increasing, but was still being checked by police measures of coercion. The Tsar's ministers still were relying on the army. Even during the first days of March, 1917, the disorders in Petrograd were being effectively quelled by troops and police. Toward the evening of the seventh, however, some regiments began to waver, and this moment can rightly be looked at as the real beginning of the Revolution. A squadron of Cossacks, near the Nicholas railway station, took sides with the populace and attacked the mounted police, cheered and acclaimed by the mob. On Sunday, the eighth, in other places in Petrograd soldiers refused to shoot at the crowd. From this moment on the Tsar's government was doomed. On the ninth, riots broke out in many barracks, a few officers were killed and several battalions marched out, going to the Duma.

By that time the Revolution was well under way; a few hours later most of the old ministers were arrested and the power of government went over to the Temporary Committee of the Duma.

Who started the Revolution during those fateful days of March? Who called out the first regiments and brought the people of Petrograd out into the streets to fight the police? We now know that it was not any individual, nor any party, nor any organization. There was *no* leadership those first three days. On one

of those nights some socialistic and radical organizations did have a party meeting, discussing the situation, but according to the unanimous testimony of participants, it seemed to them that for the moment the
government police had won out and that the time for
the Revolution had not yet come. These were the
more radical views; the liberal and conservative elements had no party meetings at all during the first
days. The soldiers in the street refused to obey orders
because they instinctively felt that the nation was
against the government and that the former and not
the latter was right. The battalions left their barracks
and marched to the Duma also without any leaders,
only instinctively feeling that something was going
on and that they could find new leaders for the moment
only in the Duma. It was quite like a huge tidal wave
that suddenly swept over the city, absolutely unconscious, but terrible in its threatening attitude. It was
a splendid chance for new leaders to step in and control this awe-inspiring movement. Unfortunately nobody was there to take the lead and unite these forces;
neither liberals nor radicals were prepared to take the
leadership. It was a brilliant chance for a Napoleon
to appear. There is no doubt but that for a time at
least the army would have followed him. The habit
of discipline was still deeply ingrained in the soldiers'
minds and obedience and discipline could have been
at least temporarily restored. At that moment a
strong man could still have enforced his will.

These fatal March days will always remain most en-
ticing material for the study of the behavior of crowds
and of the working of the group-mind. They are, too,

an important proof of how much the start of a revolution depends on the behavior of the army.

This applies just as well to the events that followed the Japanese War, when the first revolutionary rumblings were distinctly heard in Russia, and also to the present-day Bolshevik régime, when once more revolutionary events are in no way excluded on account of the frightful shortcomings of the Bolsheviki. In both cases the revolutionary outbreak depends entirely on the stand of the army. In 1905, when military defeat brought with it moral humiliation of the government, disclosing the defects of the administration, the revolutionary discontent increased tremendously; all over the country riots and uprisings were taking place. In some instances army units became demoralized and did not obey government orders; some battalions refused to quell disorders. But on the whole the army still stood firm. The demoralization affected only those troops that were returning from the Far East of Siberia, and they were only a relatively small part of the Russian army. The government had sufficient numbers of reliable troops to cope with the situation and finally did master it * ; in consequence, the Revolution did not start then, though the ideology of it and the social discontent of the Russian people were quite ripe for it.

Another striking example is the German Revolution of November, 1918, that broke out with a mutiny of the Kiel sailors and spread rapidly among other garrisons.

* Count Witte, in his "Memoirs," gives a graphic account of how the government, of which he was then the head, dealt with this dangerous situation.

The case is exactly the same with the present-day autocracy; the Bolsheviki know very well that their power depends entirely on the Red army and will last only as long as the army obeys their orders and is willing to quell uprisings and riots. A new revolution can come only in case the Red army becomes demoralized. For this reason the Bolsheviki do all they can to have the army well satisfied; they feed it and care for it as best they can and keep it in much better condition than the rest of the population, giving it sufficient rations, supplying it with ammunition left over from the Great War or produced by government factories, and endeavor to keep it constantly occupied, well knowing that leisure breeds laziness, propaganda and dissatisfaction.

Another interesting lesson that we have learned from the Russian Revolution is the fact that revolution itself does not bring with it a millennium. People are not emancipated *eo ipso* when a revolution breaks out. Rather, on the contrary, a period of worse oppression and intensified social evils might follow before the good results of a revolution begin to tell. The revolution is distinctly a destructive process; *it is the breaking up* of an antiquated political system and social order, that have lived their day but are not willing to die or give way of their own accord. Construction of a new order that would replace the destroyed one is a slow and tedious process that usually does not start from the first moment destruction is achieved. Even the latter process, that of destruction, takes often many years to be thoroughly accomplished; and while the

powerful destructive forces are in full sway, the opposite forces, those of construction, are and must remain
in abeyance.

Thus there often comes a *hiatus,* a gap, between the
old and the new order, during which the nation that is
going through a revolution only suffers—and often
worse than during the last years of the old régime.
No freedom came in Russia after the revolutionary
events of November, 1917. The people did not get the
emancipation they expected and longed for. On the
contrary, oppression even became worse than ever; no
personal freedom whatever existed; all forms of liberty
were curtailed or annihilated; the citizen had no redress
from the arbitrary actions of officials. No freedom of
personality, of press, of organization and assembly
were to be found anywhere. Men and women were
arrested, imprisoned, and executed at the slightest pre-
text and without any legal proceedings whatever. No
press, except the government papers, existed any more.
No assemblies or organizations were tolerated. And
with this there came the usual consequences bred in
such an atmosphere of political slavery: corruption,
abuses, official mismanagement, dishonesty, bribery
and so on, which only helped to arouse the suspicions
and hatred of the masses. Most unfortunately, it also
fostered a great antagonism to the educated classes.
The masses did not and could not feel that the revolution had brought them any change whatever. The people soon lost their momentary enthusiasm of the first
revolutionary days and reverted to their former state
of mind. Downcast and subservient, they were now
living in much worse physical condition than ever be-

fore. Their ways of living became crude and primitive. One would think that the Middle Ages had come back to Russia.

In this state of things there appeared a very dangerous and evil sign; namely, the spread of anti-Semitism. The masses were looking for an individual culprit, for a scapegoat or originator of all those sufferings, and many extremists (old and new, reactionaries and Bolsheviki) were whispering to them that the main culprit was the *Jew*. In consequence a great feeling of hatred began slowly to grow up, menacing and dreadful. Many pretexts were found to accuse the Jews, numerous proofs were alleged to exist of their alone having started the whole trouble and caused all the sufferings to the people. With suffering come superstitions; all such rumors were easily believed by the ignorant. So a pernicious legend grew up and spread its poison all over the country. It will prove one of the greatest difficulties that any new government will have to cope with in future regenerated Russia. The hatred against the Jews will not be easily eradicated.

Finally, there came another unexpected evil. The labor class became absolutely defenseless and powerless. One would have expected just the opposite to happen. The régime was ostensibly built for the workingmen and by them, and yet their position now became much worse than it ever had been. Exploitation of labor in the most ruthless forms was as bad as ever, but simultaneously all the institutions and guaranties of protection of labor, so carefully constructed by preceding generations, disappeared. The labor organizations were broken up; trade-unions and other professional institutions, guaranties and safeguards were smashed and torn down, because they *might* prove dangerous to the new government. The danger might have come (and probably would have come) when labor would have begun to become conscious of the failure of the new régime. This naturally would have started opposition in one form or another. Hence it had to be prevented by the Bolsheviki, and labor organizations had to be broken up in advance.

Closely related to this lesson is another one. The two extremes, reaction and Bolshevism, stand very near to one another and in all essentials are similar, in character as well as in practice. It was not quite so evident at the beginning of the Revolution, when hopes of great achievements were high and when reaction and its servants temporarily went into hiding. With the enthusiasm that reigned during those first months hardly any one could suspect or foresee that these elements of the old régime would come back so soon. As long as the Bolsheviki and their government were endeavoring to work out their communistic experiment, so strange and new, the nation was somewhat bewildered and overawed. There were many other reasons, too, for the attention of the people being directed towards other matters. The intrinsic meaning of the essentials of the new régime was thus escaping the attention of contemporaries. But as soon as the failure of the new régime became evident and Lenin with his government began to give up communism, starting concessions to capitalism and reverting to bourgeois methods of administration, the above-

mentioned resemblances between Bolshevism and reaction became evident at once.

In both cases the basic principles of government are
absolutely identical: it is a small class or group that is
imposing its rule on the vast majority of the people
exclusively by force, and maintaining its power only
by coercion. In both cases it is socially an oligarchy
and politically an autocracy, terrorizing and subduing
all elements of opposition, with only one possible difference: the methods of administration are now much
more crude and cruel than they ever were before. The
lesson that we have learned in this case is that all
autocracies and all oligarchies have to use the same
methods of government, no matter how different their
intentions may be. In all such cases it is the liberal
and progressive center that suffers most and it is just
this center that is looked upon by both extremes as the
most dangerous opponent.

Who are the most dangerous enemies of the existing
régime, according to Bolshevik authorities? Their
nearest political neighbors, the moderate socialists, who
do not accept their autocratic methods and do not believe in their communistic experiment, and the liberals
and progressive Intelligentsia, who are also fighting
the government and opposing the Bolshevik system.
Exactly the same is the case of the reactionaries,
who accuse Kerensky, Miliukov, the Jews and Masons
of having betrayed Russia (in other words, the same
social and political elements, the moderate socialists
and the liberal and progressive bourgeoisie)* and are

* The murder of V. Nabokof in Berlin, in March, 1922, was an
instance of this kind.

quite willing to coöperate even with the Bolsheviki in order to fight the moderate center. We had lately several cases, when former officials of the Tsar and other reactionaries openly advocated such coöperation. One must add, however, one excuse: the reactionaries are just as sure as all other Russians that the Bolshevik régime cannot last and their coöperation with Bolshevism is built on that hope; when Bolshevism will finally disappear, they, the reactionaries, hope to come to power.

In both cases of extreme rule, the government policies affected but little the social processes going on in the nation. The administration remained outside and above the people and had very little contact with them. One can take as a conspicuous instance the history of the nobility during the last reign of the Tsar. The nobility as a class was degenerating very fast; it was losing its social coherence. It was becoming impoverished, selling out its estates, depending entirely on the government service and assistance. The nobles were continuously asking for loans; they were given all sorts of privileges and advantages, but all in vain. The disintegration went on and could not be stopped by any artificial measures. Just the same is happening at present in Bolshevik Russia. On the one hand, we have a slow process of degeneration of the new ruling class, but, on the other, we are no more sure that the social institutions of olden days have been successfully eradicated and destroyed by the Bolsheviki.

The decadence of the Bolshevik ruling class seems to point to a coming new social readjustment. This is why so many Russians firmly believe in the possibility of a new revolutionary upheaval, though I think it is yet too early to predict such future events. We might say only that the social conditions in present-day Russia do seem to point this way, the evident degeneration of the ruling class resembling very much the epochs of such decay as preceded all revolutions. However, this is no absolute proof that revolution is the only possible outcome. Other forms of transition are by no means excluded.

The situation is much more serious as to the possible survival of some of the old social institutions of the Russian *ancien régime*. There was a time when Lenin openly boasted of having eradicated all of them. Feudalism, he said, had disappeared, monarchy was dead, the landed nobility killed, banished and ruined, the church prostrate and humiliated, and so forth. But the Bolsheviki do not at present repeat these boasts, because they themselves are no longer sure of their final victory. On the contrary, from all sides there loom up resurrected shadows of the past. The more the Bolsheviki are forced to come back to the bourgeois and capitalistic methods and principles, the stronger becomes the danger of many of the former evils eventually coming back. People begin to ask, if the bourgeoisie and capitalists come back, why not the nobility? What assurance is there against the resurrection of the former landed aristocracy, monarchy and autocracy? And the worst of it is that these forces of the old régime might find willing allies in Germany. Such fears and anticipations are of course magnified and exaggerated, but the danger is no less real and the lesson is that the two extremes do come together so closely and are so very similar both in their theory and in their practice.

One thinks involuntarily of the so-called law of the pendulum, applicable not only in physics but in sociology as well. The pendulum, having swung far to the radical left, has to come back to the reactionary right before it can stop in the liberal and progressive center, when stable social equilibrium can be attained once more.

But by far the most interesting and important lessons of the Russian Revolution will always remain the fate of the institutions of *Family* and *Property*.

According to the teachings of Bolshevism there might come, and in the end ought to come, a time when the principles of the bourgeois family life will be entirely changed and new conditions will set in. The Bolshevik leaders know very well, however, that these times are still very far distant and that it will require a long process before such a change can set in. They realize, too, that any change in this respect must come only gradually by an evolutionary development and cannot be forced on the people by coercion.

Yet, some time ago a story was being spread abroad by a few reactionaries about the supposed nationalization of women in Russia. It was used to placard the Bolshevik régime as immoral and hideous. As a matter of fact, it did more good than harm to the Bolsheviki. They had no trouble whatever to deny it and to prove that it was a lie and used it themselves as a proof of how much maligned they were by the reactionaries. Their supporters in foreign countries even at present continue to point to this story, substantiating their contention that Bolshevism in Russia is much belied by reactionaries and much better in its practice than is supposed. The story originated from a "decree" published in one of the southern provinces by local hooligans and anarchists who bragged about their achievements and preached the theory of "free love" wherever they could.

The lesson of the Russian Revolution, however, points exactly to the contrary. The family bonds and the institutions of family life have become much stronger in Russia; they are built on much sounder foundations and have a much better future assured them than ever before. This would seem to have been the natural and even necessary and unavoidable consequence of the Revolution. It came about in the following way: The Revolution, and especially Bolshevism, created much suffering, as everybody knows, and individual suffering necessarily brought about closer relations in family life. Starvation, in particular, called for tighter family bonds; brothers and sisters, children and parents were forced to go out together food-hunting and sharing the little they could procure. Suffering calls for sympathy. Who would be expected to help and assist first—a relative, a member of the same family, or a stranger and outsider? Evidently the former, whereas the latter would be estranged by jealousy and competition. In the family group the struggle for existence was easier than if it had been conducted single-handed; means of existence were always procured more easily if derived from the joint efforts of several members of one family; if one member was out of employment, the others still could get along, and so forth.

The increase and frequency of divorces in Bolshevik Russia are often cited as a proof of the decay of family life. This, however, is misleading. The few divorces are never any proof of happiness and stability of family life, or vice versa. The frequency of divorces in America, especially in some states of the Union, is notorious, and yet no country can boast of better conditions of family life than the United States.

Indeed, divorces became much easier and more frequent in Bolshevik Russia than they ever were before. The church cannot create any impediments, the government frankly does not care about them, society or caste do no longer exist; thus family life is left to its own evolution. The more important on this account are the social results. Family life not only stood the test of this terrific trial, but came out of it, as has just been said, stronger, more stable and better equipped for the struggle.

The roots of family life, whatever its historical origin may have been, are so deeply ingrained in human nature that nothing can eradicate them. The human being has to live in the family. The latter is the basic foundation of society and state. But there is more to it: moral ideas and spiritual development are the great product and achievement of civilization and constitute the progress of humanity. What is our civilization worth without them? And very much, if not everything, depends in their development on the principles imbibed by the individual in family life, in his childhood, from the care of the parents. No school, no government, nor any state can achieve this with the same ease and efficiency. The history of the Russian Revolution corroborates this in the most marked way, and in the new, stronger and better family bonds of the family life the Russian people have acquired a remarkable assurance of a more promising future.

No less important is the second lesson. Private property emerges from the Revolution also much better guaranteed and much more stable than it ever was in the Tsar's times. This is the more remarkable because the Bolshevik régime was very intense and sincere in endeavoring to abolish property. Bolshevism is communism and frankly denies private property. Accordingly, during the first months of 1918 the Bolsheviki tried to nationalize whatever they could. But just in this respect, more than anywhere else, Bolshevism failed, and failed irrevocably.

The educated people in Russia were opposed to Bolshevism from the very start, because they believed that communism could not work in practice. Many among them knew that the numerous historical attempts to establish communism had invariably failed; history taught them that communism was too much against human nature in every respect, but unfortunately the historical lessons seldom serve to any purpose, and hardly ever are learned by succeeding generations.

In 1917 the masses of the people, the peasantry at large, had not yet any clear idea of private property. For centuries they had been serfs and could not dispose freely of their property, particularly the land they tilled and lived on. The old peasant commune was effectively hampering the growth of the idea of property. The socialists and other radicals were honestly convinced that the Russian peasant would always continue to live in some form of a commune. The Bolsheviki also expected that in the beginning; in fact, this was the main hope for their whole experiment in communism.

The disappointment came at the end of the second year of their government. The peasants had grabbed the land of the former nobility and of the crown and absolutely refused to part with it. They did not want any "communal" landholding; they did not expect any communes to last any more; they did not recognize the state nor the village as communes "above" them, and they strongly insisted on *owning* the land which they had acquired and on disposing of it as they pleased, buying or selling, inheriting or exchanging. For a moment the Bolshevik government tried to coerce them and force the commune upon them, but without any success. These Bolshevik efforts were of no avail; they met with stubborn and uncompromising resistance and soon had to be given up. This was the first but really the fatal concession that Lenin had to make. It was fatal because it meant the denial of his cherished and most essential ideal, communism. It meant in addition the ultimate breakdown of his whole system, because Bolshevism without communism has no justification whatever and simply boils down to naked, shameless autocracy. He must have felt this from the very first day that he became aware that the peasants intended to hold their land in private ownership and that absolutely nothing could force them to give it up. This was the turning point of the Bolshevik régime, the start of its unavoidable decline. The régime stumbled over the idea of private property.

On the other hand, the peasants not having had a very clear idea of private property in former times also learned the lesson. After they had acquired the land which they had been hoping to get for so many generations, they did not intend to lose it again. They realized the value of private property, its meaning and purpose. In consequence the Bolshevik régime became a distinct disappointment for them. They had the promises of Lenin to secure more land for them. This was one of the cleverest and most successful slogans of 1917. It recruited many supporters to Bolshevism during the Kerensky régime. The peasants got the land, and then suddenly realized that this land after all was not theirs, that it was meant to belong to the commune, the impersonal state, far above them, and this naturally seemed to them just as bad as the Tsar's régime with its landlords and bureaucracy. Their enthusiasm for Bolshevism evaporated at once; their support disappeared and with it had to vanish the social backing and strength of the Bolshevik government. No wonder the latter became very much alarmed. They could not help themselves, however, and had to compromise, though well realizing that such a concession meant the breakdown of their innermost hopes and ideals.

Thus, in the end, the idea of private property came out of the Revolution stronger and more stable than ever. Here again, as in the institutions of family life, whatever the historical origins of private property, the human being at present cannot live without it; it is too deeply ingrained in the human nature to be eradicated by some haphazard decrees of a few fanatics who don't believe in it.

Still, the assertion that private property is so deeply ingrained in human nature that it cannot be eradicated and that it constitutes one of the most important pillars on which our social life is built, must not be taken as unqualified praise of it. Contemporary social life tends to prove that private property is not always a boon, that, on the contrary, it has many important defects and creates some conspicuous evils. But instead of simply denying it or foolishly trying to abolish it, science must study such defects and find remedies for them, eradicating the evil consequences without denying the institution itself, and governments and statesmen must build up and adopt policies that will lessen such evils and protect the people against the defects of the different forms of private property.

INDEX

A

Agent-provocateur, 137
Alexander II, 7, 10, 18, 32, 51
Alexander III, 11, 16, 17, 36, 52, 53, 101
Alexandra, Empress, 18, 19, 90, 91
Alexis, Grand Duke, 18
Allies, 113, 114, 115, 125, 127, 138
American revolution, 131
Amnesty for political prisoners, 77
Amur river, 58
Anarchy, 135
Ancien régime, 15, 21, 25, 27, 28, 57, 68, 73, 75, 92, 93, 97, 98, 102, 103, 124, 132, 133, 145, 148
Anti-Semitism, 144
Apocryphal testament, 117
Arctic coast, 117
Aristocracy, 12, 14, 15, 16, 23, 28, 33, 35, 78, 100, 148
Armistice, 128
Asef, 26, 137
Austria, 118, 119
Autocracy, 1, 2, 3, 4, 5, 6, 7, 8, 11, 12, 13, 15, 16, 17, 20, 21, 24, 27, 28, 54, 55, 56, 57, 61, 62, 63, 64, 65, 67, 68, 71, 76, 77, 83, 84, 99, 103, 108, 114, 118, 122, 123, 129, 135, 137, 142, 146, 153

B

Balkan Slavs, 10
Baltic, 17, 18, 126
Bill of rights, 74
Bismarck, 118, 126
Blockade, 88
Bolshevik socialists, 96, 97, 98, 99, 100, 115, 119, 121, 124, 125, 128, 142, 145, 146, 147, 148, 149

Bolshevism, 30, 42, 46, 47, 48, 97, 99, 101, 104, 105, 106, 120, 123, 127, 128, 129, 133, 134, 135, 141, 145, 146, 149, 150, 151, 152, 153, 154
Border-states, 118, 126
Bourbons, 6
Bourgeoisie, 29, 30, 45, 46, 49, 86, 92, 97, 98, 99, 145, 146, 148
Brest-Litovsk, 125, 126
British empire, *see* Great Britain
Bureaucracy, 12, 13, 14, 15, 16, 20, 22, 23, 24, 25, 26, 27, 28, 32, 52, 61, 63, 66, 73, 78, 79, 97, 100, 118, 154

C

Cabinet system of government, 75, 76
Cadet party, 71, 78
Carier, 94
Censorship, 73
Chèradame, A., 69
China, 58, 59, 60, 63
Commune, village, 38, 39, 40, 44, 45, 47, 153
Communism, 30, 38, 42, 47, 48, 49, 96, 98, 99, 100, 101, 122, 124, 145, 152, 153
Conservatives, 32, 96, 134, 140
Constitution, 7, 8, 20, 21, 22, 24, 27, 73, 78
Constitutional-Democratic party, 71, 77
Constitutionalism, 8, 9, 22, 25, 50, 68, 73, 74, 75, 77, 114
Court, Russian, 17, 18, 19, 23, 33, 66, 73, 75, 76, 78, 90
Courts-of-Law, 7
Cracow, 118, 119
Crimean War, 6, 32, 51, 115
Crowd psychology, 80

157

D

Danton, 94
December revolt, 6
"Defeatist" movement, 115, 116
Dictatorship of the Proletariat, 99
Divorces, 151
Dogger Bank, 111
Duma, 21, 22, 71, 77, 78, 88, 91, 92, 139, 140
Durnovo, P., 76

E

Economic expansion, 58, 65
Economists, 44, 45
Educated people, 3, 9, 37, 49, 50, 64, 67, 87, 143
Egypt, 109
Empire of the Tsars, 97, 113
Extremists, 116, 120

F

Family, 149
Family life, 41, 149, 150, 151, 154
Far East, 25, 58, 59, 61, 62, 63, 70
Finland, 27, 110, 111, 116, 117, 118, 124
"Fists," 43
Foodstuffs, 47, 58, 88, 91, 95, 135
France, 29, 31, 59, 70, 76, 77, 84
Franco-Russian alliance, 70
French courts, 7
French Revolution, 29, 30, 92, 94, 131, 132
French Terror, 132
"From Heaven to Hell," 94

G

Galacia, 118, 119
Gendarmerie, 26
Gentry, 53, 78
German general staff, 104, 117, 119, 120, 121, 122, 123
German revolution of Nov., 1918, 141
Germany, 17, 18, 57, 69, 70, 86, 89, 90, 104, 105, 106, 107, 108, 112, 113, 119, 121, 123, 125, 127, 128, 129
Governors, 52, 54
Grand dukes, 18, 19, 91
Great Britain, 59, 61, 107, 108, 109, 110
Great Britain, colonies, 107, 108, 109

H

Helferich, Vice-Chancellor, 126
Helsingfors, 111
History, lessons of, 72, 130
Hoffmann, 117, 121, 123
Hohenzollern, house of, 113

I

Imperial family, 10, 17, 18, 23, 60, 86, 90, 112
Imperialism, 25, 57, 58, 60, 61, 62, 63, 65, 69
Indemnity, 69
India, 109
"Intelligence" organizations, 118
Intelligentsia, 16, 37, 41, 49, 55, 72, 87, 146

J

Japan, 20, 27, 36, 43, 58, 60, 61, 64, 65, 67, 68, 69, 70, 110, 111
Jews, 105, 144, 146
Joffe, 128
John Grafton, the, 110
Judiciary, 52

K

Kaiser (Wilhelm II), 70, 108, 112
Kamchatka, 58
Kamenev, 119
Kerensky, 46, 94, 95, 96, 97, 98, 123, 124, 146, 154
Kiao-chow, 59
Kiel, 141
Kienthal, 115
Koolaki, 43
Korea, 58, 60, 61
Kovalevsky, M., 39, 75
Krivosheïne, 27

Kropotkin, 114
Kuropatkin, General, 66, 68
Kwangchow-wan, 59

L

Labor, 21, 30, 86, 93, 96, 100, 101,
 144, 145
Land act of 1906, 43
Land hunger, 31, 34, 37, 46, 54,
 96.
Land ownership, 34, 36, 38, 42,
 44, 46, 48, 51, 54, 77, 95, 153
"Leases" of territory, 59
Lenin, 94, 95, 115, 119, 121, 122,
 123, 124, 128, 129, 145, 148, 153,
 154
Letts, 35
Liberal center parties, 77, 78
Liberal movement, 7, 8, 20, 21,
 32, 33, 74, 76, 101, 115, 134, 149
Liberals, 74, 75, 76, 77, 89, 92, 94,
 96, 140, 146
Liberty, 95
Li-Hung-Chang, 59
Little Russians, 119
Loans, 59, 76, 77
Ludendorff, 104, 108, 117, 120,
 121, 123, 129
Lvov, Prince, 75, 94, 96

M

McDougall, W., 81
Manchuria, 20, 58, 60, 61, 66, 68,
 71
Marat, 94
Markets, 58, 59, 61, 62, 126, 127
Martin, E. D., 81, 83, 94, 97
Masons, 146
Miliukov, P. N., 26, 34, 39, 75,
 89, 94, 146
Mir, 38, 39, 40, 44, 45, 48
Mirabeau, 94
Mirbach, Count, 125, 126, 127
Mongol, 2
Moscow, 12, 19, 39, 88, 125, 126

N

Nabokof, V., 146
Napoleon, 6

Nationalistic movement, 23
Nationalization of women, 149
Nicholas I, 8, 17, 90
Nicholas II, 12, 16, 18, 71, 101
Nicholas, Grand Duke, 19
Nietzsche, 82
Nobility, 12, 13, 23, 32, 33, 35, 43,
 53, 54, 72, 78, 97, 100, 147, 148,
 153
Non-Slavic peoples, 25, 26, 87,
 113, 114, 118
North Sea, 111
Norway, 117
Noske, G., 129
November revolution, 100

O

Octobrist party, 78, 79
Oligarchy, 99, 146
Ooprava, 52

P

Pacifism, 67
Parliament, 7, 22, 71, 88
Peace, 67, 68, 95, 125
Peasants, 8, 29, 30, 31, 33, 34, 35,
 36, 40, 41, 43, 44, 45, 46, 47, 48,
 49, 50, 51, 54, 55, 72, 77, 93, 95,
 96, 100, 152, 153, 154
Peter the Great, 117
Petrograd, 20, 22, 88, 93, 124, 139
Philippe, 19
Plehanoff, 114
Poland, 27, 118
Police, 23, 25, 26, 51, 52, 77, 78,
 92, 114, 116, 128, 136, 137, 139
Political system, 64
Pooley, A. M., 111
Populists, 38
Port Arthur, 59, 60, 61, 65
Portsmouth Peace, 57, 69, 73
Powers, great, 59, 61
Progressives, 32, 73, 92, 94, 146
Proletariat, 99, 122
Propaganda, 86, 87, 102, 106, 109,
 110, 111, 115, 116, 117, 118, 119,
 124, 127, 128, 129, 133, 139
Property, 41, 43, 48, 49, 72, 149,
 152, 154, 155
Provincial administration, 51, 53

Provisional government of March, 1917, 92, 94, 96, 98
Psychological phenomena of the crowd, 80

R

Racial questions, 109
Radek, K., 120, 121
Radicalism, 11, 67, 95, 116, 118, 120
Rasputin, 19, 90
Reactionaries, 8, 9, 10, 22, 33, 73, 74, 76, 77, 78, 79, 134, 145, 146, 147, 149, 150
Red army, 142
Red Cross, 71
Reform, 7, 8, 20, 33, 37, 52, 53, 57, 67, 68, 69, 71, 72, 78, 79, 93, 115
Requisitions, 47
Revolt, definition of, 82
Revolution, definition of, 82, 83, 84
Robespierre, 94
Roman empire, 131
Romanoff, house of, 112, 113
Russia, foreign relations, 57
Russian army, 6, 23, 39, 64, 66, 67, 68, 71, 113, 120, 123, 125, 136, 137, 138
Russian exiles, 114, 115, 119, 123
Russian navy, 60, 65, 93, 111, 124
Russian revolution, 1, 13, 20, 21, 27, 29, 30, 31, 42, 46, 48, 49, 50, 56, 72, 79, 81, 85, 92, 93, 94, 95, 101, 104, 105, 117, 121, 129, 131, 132, 133, 134, 135, 137, 139, 140, 142, 145, 149, 150, 152
Russo-Japanese war, 20, 56, 57, 64, 66, 70, 71, 110, 115, 141

S

St. Petersburg, 66
Sakhalin, island of, 69
Samara, province of, 43
Scandinavia, 116, 117
Scheinkonstitutionalismus, 21
"Sealed train," 120
Self-government, 50, 51, 53
Serfs, 7, 10, 31, 32, 33, 34, 40, 41, 51, 54, 152

Serge, Grand Duke, 19
Shimonoseki, 59
Shipov, Prince, 75
Siberia, 63, 141
Sino-Japanese war, 58
Slavophiles, 39
Slavs, 10
Social life, 4
Social psychology, 81
"Social" revolution, 46
Socialism, 98, 118
Socialists, 38, 41, 42, 67, 77, 78, 93, 96, 116, 146, 153
Soviet government, 38, 42
Soviets, 96
Spy systems, 86
Starvation, 150
Stolypin, 24, 37, 43, 77, 78, 137
Sturmer, prime minister, 89
Suffrage, 51, 71, 78
Sukhomlinoff, General, 26
Sveaborg, fortress of, 111
Sweden, 116, 117, 118, 124
Switzerland, 114, 115, 119, 120

T

Tambov, province of, 43
Tartars, 12
Taxation, 34, 39, 40, 77
Tchekhov, A., 36
Trotzky, 94, 95, 124, 125
Trubetzkoi, Prince, 75
Tsar, 5, 6, 7, 9, 10, 12, 14, 15, 16, 17, 18, 19, 20, 22, 23, 25, 28, 32, 33, 39, 47, 60, 62, 66, 70, 71, 73, 74, 76, 78, 79, 87, 90, 91, 92, 103, 112, 113, 114, 116, 117, 119, 135, 138, 147, 154
Tsusima, 20

U

Ukraine, 27, 119
Ukrainophiles, 119
Union sacré, 89, 114
United States, 151

W

Wei-hai-Wei, 59
Western Europe, 11, 15, 114
Wilhelm II, 70, 108, 112
Williams, Harold W., 20

Williams, J. M , 81
Witte, Count, 21, 62, 69, 73, 74, 75, 76, 77, 141
World War, 11, 19, 45, 70, 79, 81, 85, 86, 89, 112, 116, 137, 142

Y

Yakutsk, 58

Yalu river, 60

Z

Zemskii Nachalniki, 52, 54
Zemstvos, 50, 51, 52, 53, 54, 71
Zilliacus, K., 111
Zimmerwaldt, 115, 116
Zinoviev, 119